Countryside and Rights of Way Act 2000

CHAPTER 37

ARRANGEMENT OF SECTIONS

PART I

ACCESS TO THE COUNTRYSIDE

CHAPTER I

RIGHT OF ACCESS

General

Miscellaneous provisions relating to right of access

PART III

NATURE CONSERVATION AND WILDLIFE PROTECTION

The Nature Conservancy Council for England

Biological diversity

Sites of special scientific interest

Ramsar sites

Limestone pavement orders

Countryside and Rights of Way Act 2000

2000 CHAPTER 37

An Act to make new provision for public access to the countryside; to amend the law relating to public rights of way; to enable traffic regulation orders to be made for the purpose of conserving an area's natural beauty; to make provision with respect to the driving of mechanically propelled vehicles elsewhere than on roads; to amend the law relating to nature conservation and the protection of wildlife; to make further provision with respect to areas of outstanding natural beauty; and for connected purposes. [30th November 2000]

BE IT ENACTED by the Queen's most Excellent Majesty, by and with the advice and consent of the Lords Spiritual and Temporal, and Commons, in this present Parliament assembled, and by the authority of the same, as follows:—

PART I

ACCESS TO THE COUNTRYSIDE

CHAPTER I

RIGHT OF ACCESS

General

1.—(1) In this Part "access land" means any land which—

(a) is shown as open country on a map in conclusive form issued by the appropriate countryside body for the purposes of this Part,

(b) is shown on such a map as registered common land,

(c) is registered common land in any area outside Inner London for which no such map relating to registered common land has been issued,

(d) is situated more than 600 metres above sea level in any area for which no such map relating to open country has been issued, or

Principal definitions for Part I.

(e) is dedicated for the purposes of this Part under section 16,

but does not (in any of those cases) include excepted land or land which is treated by section 15(1) as being accessible to the public apart from this Act.

(2) In this Part—

"access authority"—

(a) in relation to land in a National Park, means the National Park authority, and

(b) in relation to any other land, means the local highway authority in whose area the land is situated;

"the appropriate countryside body" means—

(a) in relation to England, the Countryside Agency, and

(b) in relation to Wales, the Countryside Council for Wales;

"excepted land" means land which is for the time being of any of the descriptions specified in Part I of Schedule 1, those descriptions having effect subject to Part II of that Schedule;

"mountain" includes, subject to the following definition, any land situated more than 600 metres above sea level;

"mountain, moor, heath or down" does not include land which appears to the appropriate countryside body to consist of improved or semi-improved grassland;

"open country" means land which—

(a) appears to the appropriate countryside body to consist wholly or predominantly of mountain, moor, heath or down, and

(b) is not registered common land.

(3) In this Part "registered common land" means—

1965 c. 64.

(a) land which is registered as common land under the Commons Registration Act 1965 (in this section referred to as "the 1965 Act") and whose registration under that Act has become final, or

(b) subject to subsection (4), land which fell within paragraph (a) on the day on which this Act is passed or at any time after that day but has subsequently ceased to be registered as common land under the 1965 Act on the register of common land in which it was included being amended by reason of the land having ceased to be common land within the meaning of that Act.

(4) Subsection (3)(b) does not apply where—

(a) the amendment of the register of common land was made in pursuance of an application made before the day on which this Act is passed, or

(b) the land ceased to be common land by reason of the exercise of—

(i) any power of compulsory purchase, of appropriation or of sale which is conferred by an enactment,

(ii) any power so conferred under which land may be made common land within the meaning of the 1965 Act in substitution for other land.

2.—(1) Any person is entitled by virtue of this subsection to enter and remain on any access land for the purposes of open-air recreation, if and so long as—

Rights of public in relation to access land.

> (a) he does so without breaking or damaging any wall, fence, hedge, stile or gate, and
>
> (b) he observes the general restrictions in Schedule 2 and any other restrictions imposed in relation to the land under Chapter II.

(2) Subsection (1) has effect subject to subsections (3) and (4) and to the provisions of Chapter II.

(3) Subsection (1) does not entitle a person to enter or be on any land, or do anything on any land, in contravention of any prohibition contained in or having effect under any enactment, other than an enactment contained in a local or private Act.

(4) If a person becomes a trespasser on any access land by failing to comply with—

> (a) subsection (1)(a),
>
> (b) the general restrictions in Schedule 2, or
>
> (c) any other restrictions imposed in relation to the land under Chapter II,

he may not, within 72 hours after leaving that land, exercise his right under subsection (1) to enter that land again or to enter other land in the same ownership.

(5) In this section "owner", in relation to any land which is subject to a farm business tenancy within the meaning of the Agricultural Tenancies Act 1995 or a tenancy to which the Agricultural Holdings Act 1986 applies, means the tenant under that tenancy, and "ownership" shall be construed accordingly.

1995 c. 8.
1986 c. 5.

3.—(1) The Secretary of State (as respects England) or the National Assembly for Wales (as respects Wales) may by order amend the definition of "open country" in section 1(2) so as to include a reference to coastal land or to coastal land of any description.

Power to extend to coastal land.

(2) An order under this section may—

> (a) make consequential amendments of other provisions of this Part, and
>
> (b) modify the provisions of this Part in their application to land which is open country merely because it is coastal land.

(3) In this section "coastal land" means—

> (a) the foreshore, and
>
> (b) land adjacent to the foreshore (including in particular any cliff, bank, barrier, dune, beach or flat which is adjacent to the foreshore).

Maps

4—(1) It shall be the duty of the Countryside Agency to prepare, in respect of England outside Inner London, maps which together show—

Duty to prepare maps.

> (a) all registered common land, and
>
> (b) all open country.

(2) It shall be the duty of the Countryside Council for Wales to prepare, in respect of Wales, maps which together show—

(a) all registered common land, and

(b) all open country.

(3) Subsections (1) and (2) have effect subject to the following provisions of this section and to the provisions of sections 5 to 9.

(4) A map prepared under this section must distinguish between open country and registered common land, but need not distinguish between different categories of open country.

(5) In preparing a map under this section, the appropriate countryside body—

(a) may determine not to show as open country areas of open country which are so small that the body consider that their inclusion would serve no useful purpose, and

(b) may determine that any boundary of an area of open country is to be treated as coinciding with a particular physical feature (whether the effect is to include other land as open country or to exclude part of an area of open country).

Publication of draft maps.

5. The appropriate countryside body shall—

(a) issue in draft form any map prepared by them under section 4,

(b) consider any representations received by them within the prescribed period with respect to the showing of, or the failure to show, any area of land on the map as registered common land or as open country,

(c) confirm the map with or without modifications,

(d) if the map has been confirmed without modifications, issue it in provisional form, and

(e) if the map has been confirmed with modifications, prepare a map incorporating the modifications, and issue that map in provisional form.

Appeal against map after confirmation.

6.—(1) Any person having an interest in any land may appeal—

(a) in the case of land in England, to the Secretary of State, or

(b) in the case of land in Wales, to the National Assembly for Wales,

against the showing of that land on a map in provisional form as registered common land or as open country.

(2) An appeal relating to the showing of any land as registered common land may be brought only on the ground that the land is not registered common land.

(3) An appeal relating to the showing of any land as open country may be brought only on the ground that—

(a) the land does not consist wholly or predominantly of mountain, moor, heath or down, and

(b) to the extent that the appropriate countryside body have exercised their discretion under section 4(5)(b) to treat land which is not open country as forming part of an area of open country, the body ought not to have done so.

(4) On an appeal under this section, the Secretary of State or the National Assembly for Wales may—

    (a) approve the whole or part of the map which is the subject of the appeal, with or without modifications, or

    (b) require the appropriate countryside body to prepare under section 4 a new map relating to all or part of the area covered by the map which is the subject of the appeal.

7.—(1) Before determining an appeal under section 6, the Secretary of State or the National Assembly for Wales may, if he or it thinks fit—   Appeal procedure.

    (a) cause the appeal to take, or continue in, the form of a hearing, or

    (b) cause a local inquiry to be held;

and the appeal authority shall act as mentioned in paragraph (a) or (b) if a request is made by either party to the appeal to be heard with respect to the appeal.

(2) Subsections (2) to (5) of section 250 of the Local Government Act 1972 (local inquiries: evidence and costs) apply to a hearing or local inquiry held under this section as they apply to a local inquiry held under that section, but as if—   1972 c. 70.

    (a) references in that section to the person appointed to hold the inquiry were references to the Secretary of State or the National Assembly for Wales, and

    (b) references in that section to the Minister causing an inquiry to be held were references to the Secretary of State or the Assembly.

(3) Where—

    (a) for the purposes of an appeal under section 6, the Secretary of State or the National Assembly for Wales is required by subsection (1)—

        (i) to cause the appeal to take, or continue in, the form of a hearing, or

        (ii) to cause a local inquiry to be held, and

    (b) the inquiry or hearing does not take place, and

    (c) if it had taken place, the Secretary of State or the Assembly or a person appointed by the Secretary of State or the Assembly would have had power to make an order under section 250(5) of the Local Government Act 1972 requiring any party to pay the costs of the other party,

the power to make such an order may be exercised, in relation to costs incurred for the purposes of the inquiry or hearing, as if it had taken place.

(4) This section has effect subject to section 8.

8.—(1) The Secretary of State or the National Assembly for Wales may—   Power of Secretary of State or Assembly to delegate functions relating to appeals.

    (a) appoint any person to exercise on his or its behalf, with or without payment, the function of determining—

        (i) an appeal under section 6, or

        (ii) any matter involved in such an appeal, or

(b) refer any matter involved in such an appeal to such person as the Secretary of State or the Assembly may appoint for the purpose, with or without payment.

(2) Schedule 3 has effect with respect to appointments under subsection (1)(a).

Maps in conclusive form.

9.—(1) Where—

(a) the time within which any appeal under section 6 may be brought in relation to a map in provisional form has expired and no appeal has been brought, or

(b) every appeal brought under that section in relation to a map has—

(i) been determined by the map or part of it being approved without modifications, or

(ii) been withdrawn,

the appropriate countryside body shall issue the map (or the part or parts of it that have been approved without modifications) as a map in conclusive form.

(2) Where—

(a) every appeal brought under section 6 in relation to a map in provisional form has been determined or withdrawn, and

(b) on one or more appeals, the map or any part of it has been approved with modifications,

the appropriate countryside body shall prepare a map which covers the area covered by the map in provisional form (or the part or parts of the map in provisional form that have been approved with or without modifications) and incorporates the modifications, and shall issue it as a map in conclusive form.

(3) Where either of the conditions in subsection (1)(a) and (b) is satisfied in relation to any part of a map in provisional form, the Secretary of State (as respects England) or the National Assembly for Wales (as respects Wales) may direct the relevant countryside body to issue that part of the map as a map in conclusive form.

(4) Where on an appeal under section 6 part of a map in provisional form has been approved with modifications but the condition in subsection (2)(a) is not yet satisfied, the Secretary of State (as respects England) or the National Assembly for Wales (as respects Wales) may direct the relevant countryside body to issue a map which covers the area covered by that part of the map in provisional form and incorporates the modifications, and to issue it as a map in conclusive form.

(5) Where a map in conclusive form has been issued in compliance with a direction under subsection (3) or (4), subsections (1) and (2) shall have effect as if any reference to the map in provisional form were a reference to the part not affected by the direction.

(6) A document purporting to be certified on behalf of the appropriate countryside body to be a copy of or of any part of a map in conclusive form issued by that body for the purposes of this Part shall be receivable in evidence and shall be deemed, unless the contrary is shown, to be such a copy.

10.—(1) Where the appropriate countryside body have issued a map in   conclusive form in respect of any area, it shall be the duty of the body from time to time, on a review under this section, to consider—

    (a) whether any land shown on that map as open country or registered common land is open country or registered common land at the time of the review, and

    (b) whether any land in that area which is not so shown ought to be so shown.

(2) A review under this section must be undertaken—

    (a) in the case of the first review, not more than ten years after the issue of the map in conclusive form, and

    (b) in the case of subsequent reviews, not more than ten years after the previous review.

(3) Regulations may amend paragraphs (a) and (b) of subsection (2) by substituting for the period for the time being specified in either of those paragraphs such other period as may be specified in the regulations.

11.—(1) Regulations may make provision supplementing the   provisions of sections 4 to 10.

(2) Regulations under this section may in particular make provision with respect to—

    (a) the scale on which maps are to be prepared,

    (b) the manner and form in which they are to be prepared and issued,

    (c) consultation with access authorities, local access forums and other persons on maps in draft form,

    (d) the steps to be taken for informing the public of the issue of maps in draft form, provisional form or conclusive form,

    (e) the manner in which maps in draft form, provisional form or conclusive form are to be published or to be made available for inspection,

    (f) the period within which and the manner in which representations on a map in draft form may be made to the appropriate countryside body,

    (g) the confirmation of a map under section 5(c),

    (h) the period within which and manner in which appeals under section 6 are to be brought,

    (i) the advertising of such an appeal,

    (j) the manner in which such appeals are to be considered,

    (k) the procedure to be followed on a review under section 10, including the issue of maps in draft form, provisional form and conclusive form on a review, and

    (l) the correction by the appropriate countryside body of minor errors or omissions in maps.

(3) Regulations made by virtue of subsection (2)(b) or (e) may authorise or require a map to be prepared, issued, published or made available for inspection in electronic form, but must require any map in electronic form to be capable of being reproduced in printed form.

(4) Regulations made by virtue of subsection (2)(k) may provide for any of the provisions of this Chapter relating to appeals to apply (with or without modifications) in relation to an appeal against a map issued in provisional form on a review.

Rights and liabilities of owners and occupiers

Effect of right of access on rights and liabilities of owners.

12.—(1) The operation of section 2(1) in relation to any access land does not increase the liability, under any enactment not contained in this Act or under any rule of law, of a person interested in the access land or any adjoining land in respect of the state of the land or of things done or omitted to be done on the land.

(2) Any restriction arising under a covenant or otherwise as to the use of any access land shall have effect subject to the provisions of this Part, and any liability of a person interested in any access land in respect of such a restriction is limited accordingly.

(3) For the purposes of any enactment or rule of law as to the circumstances in which the dedication of a highway or the grant of an easement may be presumed, or may be established by prescription, the use by the public or by any person of a way across land in the exercise of the right conferred by section 2(1) is to be disregarded.

(4) The use of any land by the inhabitants of any locality for the purposes of open-air recreation in the exercise of the right conferred by section 2(1) is to be disregarded in determining whether the land has become a town or village green.

Occupiers' liability.
1957 c. 31.

13.—(1) In section 1 of the Occupiers' Liability Act 1957 (liability in tort: preliminary), for subsection (4) there is substituted—

"(4) A person entering any premises in exercise of rights conferred by virtue of—

(a) section 2(1) of the Countryside and Rights of Way Act 2000, or

1949 c. 97.

(b) an access agreement or order under the National Parks and Access to the Countryside Act 1949,

is not, for the purposes of this Act, a visitor of the occupier of the premises."

1984 c. 3.

(2) In section 1 of the Occupiers' Liability Act 1984 (duty of occupier to persons other than his visitors), after subsection (6) there is inserted—

"(6A) At any time when the right conferred by section 2(1) of the Countryside and Rights of Way Act 2000 is exercisable in relation to land which is access land for the purposes of Part I of that Act, an occupier of the land owes (subject to subsection (6C) below) no duty by virtue of this section to any person in respect of—

(a) a risk resulting from the existence of any natural feature of the landscape, or any river, stream, ditch or pond whether or not a natural feature, or

(b) a risk of that person suffering injury when passing over, under or through any wall, fence or gate, except by proper use of the gate or of a stile.

(6B) For the purposes of subsection (6A) above, any plant, shrub or tree, of whatever origin, is to be regarded as a natural feature of the landscape.

(6C) Subsection (6A) does not prevent an occupier from owing a duty by virtue of this section in respect of any risk where the danger concerned is due to anything done by the occupier—

    (a) with the intention of creating that risk, or

    (b) being reckless as to whether that risk is created."

(3) After section 1 of that Act there is inserted—

"Special considerations relating to access land.   1A. In determining whether any, and if so what, duty is owed by virtue of section 1 by an occupier of land at any time when the right conferred by section 2(1) of the Countryside and Rights of Way Act 2000 is exercisable in relation to the land, regard is to be had, in particular, to—

    (a) the fact that the existence of that right ought not to place an undue burden (whether financial or otherwise) on the occupier,

    (b) the importance of maintaining the character of the countryside, including features of historic, traditional or archaeological interest, and

    (c) any relevant guidance given under section 20 of that Act."

14.—(1) If any person places or maintains—

    (a) on or near any access land, or

    (b) on or near a way leading to any access land,

a notice containing any false or misleading information likely to deter the public from exercising the right conferred by section 2(1), he is liable on summary conviction to a fine not exceeding level 1 on the standard scale.

Offence of displaying on access land notices deterring public use.

(2) The court before whom a person is convicted of an offence under subsection (1) may, in addition to or in substitution for the imposition of a fine, order him to remove the notice in respect of which he is convicted within such period, not being less than four days, as may be specified in the order.

(3) A person who fails to comply with an order under subsection (2) is guilty of a further offence and liable on summary conviction to a fine not exceeding level 3 on the standard scale.

Access under other enactments or by dedication

15.—(1) For the purposes of section 1(1), land is to be treated as being accessible to the public apart from this Act at any time if, but only if, at that time—

Rights of access under other enactments.

    (a) section 193 of the Law of Property Act 1925 (rights of the public over commons and waste lands) applies to it,   *1925 c. 20.*

    (b) by virtue of a local or private Act or a scheme made under Part I of the Commons Act 1899 (as read with subsection (2)), members of the public have a right of access to it at all times for the purposes of open-air recreation (however described),   *1899 c. 30.*

PART I
CHAPTER I

1949 c. 97.

(c) an access agreement or access order under Part V of the National Parks and Access to the Countryside Act 1949 is in force with respect to it, or

1979 c. 46.

(d) the public have access to it under subsection (1) of section 19 of the Ancient Monuments and Archaeological Areas Act 1979 (public access to monuments under public control) or would have access to it under that subsection but for any provision of subsections (2) to (9) of that section.

1899 c. 30.

(2) Where a local or private Act or a scheme made under Part I of the Commons Act 1899 confers on the inhabitants of a particular district or neighbourhood (however described) a right of access to any land for the purposes of open-air recreation (however described), the right of access exercisable by those inhabitants in relation to that land is by virtue of this subsection exercisable by members of the public generally.

Dedication of land as access land.

16.—(1) Subject to the provisions of this section, a person who, in respect of any land, holds—

(a) the fee simple absolute in possession, or

(b) a legal term of years absolute of which not less than 90 years remain unexpired,

may, by taking such steps as may be prescribed, dedicate the land for the purposes of this Part, whether or not it would be access land apart from this section.

(2) Where any person other than the person making the dedication holds—

(a) any leasehold interest in any of the land to be dedicated, or

(b) such other interest in any of that land as may be prescribed,

the dedication must be made jointly with that other person, in such manner as may be prescribed, or with his consent, given in such manner as may be prescribed.

(3) In relation to a dedication under this section by virtue of subsection (1)(b), the reference in subsection (2)(a) to a leasehold interest does not include a reference to a leasehold interest superior to that of the person making the dedication.

(4) A dedication made under this section by virtue of subsection (1)(b) shall have effect only for the remainder of the term held by the person making the dedication.

1967 c. 10.

(5) Schedule 2 to the Forestry Act 1967 (power for tenant for life and others to enter into forestry dedication covenants) applies to dedications under this section as it applies to forestry dedication covenants.

(6) Regulations may—

(a) prescribe the form of any instrument to be used for the purposes of this section,

(b) enable a dedication under this section to include provision removing or relaxing any of the general restrictions in Schedule 2 in relation to any of the land to which the dedication relates,

(c) enable a dedication previously made under this section to be amended by the persons by whom a dedication could be made, so as to remove or relax any of those restrictions in relation to any of the land to which the dedication relates, and

(d) require any dedication under this section, or any amendment of such a dedication by virtue of paragraph (c), to be notified to the appropriate countryside body and to the access authority.

(7) A dedication under this section is irrevocable and, subject to subsection (4), binds successive owners and occupiers of, and other persons interested in, the land to which it relates, but nothing in this section prevents any land from becoming excepted land.

(8) A dedication under this section is a local land charge.

Miscellaneous provisions relating to right of access

17.—(1) An access authority may, as respects access land in their area, make byelaws—   Byelaws.

(a) for the preservation of order,

(b) for the prevention of damage to the land or anything on or in it, and

(c) for securing that persons exercising the right conferred by section 2(1) so behave themselves as to avoid undue interference with the enjoyment of the land by other persons.

(2) Byelaws under this section may relate to all the access land in the area of the access authority or only to particular land.

(3) Before making byelaws under this section, the access authority shall consult—

(a) the appropriate countryside body, and

(b) any local access forum established for an area to which the byelaws relate.

(4) Byelaws under this section shall not interfere—

(a) with the exercise of any public right of way,

(b) with any authority having under any enactment functions relating to the land to which the byelaws apply, or

(c) with the running of a telecommunications code system or the exercise of any right conferred by or in accordance with the telecommunications code on the running of any such system.

(5) Sections 236 to 238 of the Local Government Act 1972 (which   1972 c. 70. relate to the procedure for making byelaws, authorise byelaws to impose fines not exceeding level 2 on the standard scale, and provide for the proof of byelaws in legal proceedings) apply to all byelaws under this section whether or not the authority making them is a local authority within the meaning of that Act.

(6) The confirming authority in relation to byelaws made under this section is—

(a) as respects England, the Secretary of State, and

(b) as respects Wales, the National Assembly for Wales.

(7) Byelaws under this section relating to any land—

    (a) may not be made unless the land is access land or the access authority are satisfied that it is likely to become access land, and

    (b) may not be confirmed unless the land is access land.

(8) Any access authority having power under this section to make byelaws also have power to enforce byelaws made by them; and any county council or district or parish council may enforce byelaws made under this section by another authority as respects land in the area of the council.

Wardens.

18.—(1) An access authority or a district council may appoint such number of persons as may appear to the authority making the appointment to be necessary or expedient, to act as wardens as respects access land in their area.

(2) As respects access land in an area for which there is a local access forum, an access authority shall, before they first exercise the power under subsection (1) and thereafter from time to time, consult the local access forum about the exercise of that power.

(3) Wardens may be appointed under subsection (1) for the following purposes—

    (a) to secure compliance with byelaws under section 17 and with the general restrictions in Schedule 2 and any other restrictions imposed under Chapter II,

    (b) to enforce any exclusion imposed under Chapter II,

    (c) in relation to the right conferred by section 2(1), to advise and assist the public and persons interested in access land,

    (d) to perform such other duties (if any) in relation to access land as the authority appointing them may determine.

(4) For the purpose of exercising any function conferred on him by or under this section, a warden appointed under subsection (1) may enter upon any access land.

(5) A warden appointed under subsection (1) shall, if so required, produce evidence of his authority before entering any access land in the exercise of the power conferred by subsection (4), and shall also produce evidence of his authority while he remains on the access land, if so required by any person.

(6) Except as provided by subsection (4), this section does not authorise a warden appointed under subsection (1), on land in which any person other than the authority who appointed him has an interest, to do anything which apart from this section would be actionable at that person's suit by virtue of that interest.

Notices indicating boundaries, etc.

19.—(1) An access authority may erect and maintain—

    (a) notices indicating the boundaries of access land and excepted land, and

    (b) notices informing the public of—

        (i) the effect of the general restrictions in Schedule 2,

        (ii) the exclusion or restriction under Chapter II of access by virtue of section 2(1) to any land, and

(iii) any other matters relating to access land or to access by virtue of section 2(1) which the access authority consider appropriate.

(2) In subsection (1)(b)(ii), the reference to the exclusion or restriction of access by virtue of section 2(1) is to be interpreted in accordance with section 21(2) and (3).

(3) Before erecting a notice on any land under subsection (1) the access authority shall, if reasonably practicable, consult the owner or occupier of the land.

(4) An access authority may also, as respects any access land in their area, defray or contribute towards, or undertake to defray or contribute towards, expenditure incurred or to be incurred in relation to the land by any person in displaying such notices as are mentioned in subsection (1)(a) and (b).

20.—(1) In relation to England, it shall be the duty of the Countryside Agency to issue, and from time to time revise, a code of conduct for the guidance of persons exercising the right conferred by section 2(1) and of persons interested in access land, and to take such other steps as appear to them expedient for securing— Codes of conduct and other information.

(a) that the public are informed of the situation and extent of, and means of access to, access land, and

(b) that the public and persons interested in access land are informed of their respective rights and obligations—

(i) under this Part, and

(ii) with regard to public rights of way on, and nature conservation in relation to, access land.

(2) In relation to Wales, it shall be the duty of the Countryside Council for Wales to issue, and from time to time revise, a code of conduct for the guidance of persons exercising the right conferred by section 2(1) and of persons interested in access land, and to take such other steps as appear to them expedient for securing the results mentioned in paragraphs (a) and (b) of subsection (1).

(3) A code of conduct issued by the Countryside Agency or the Countryside Council for Wales may include provisions in pursuance of subsection (1) or (2) and in pursuance of section 86(1) of the National Parks and Access to the Countryside Act 1949. 1949 c. 97.

(4) The powers conferred by subsections (1) and (2) include power to contribute towards expenses incurred by other persons.

CHAPTER II

EXCLUSION OR RESTRICTION OF ACCESS

21.—(1) References in this Chapter to the exclusion or restriction of access to any land by virtue of section 2(1) are to be interpreted in accordance with subsections (2) and (3). Interpretation of Chapter II.

(2) A person excludes access by virtue of subsection (1) of section 2 to any land where he excludes the application of that subsection in relation to that land.

(3) A person restricts access by virtue of subsection (1) of section 2 to any land where he provides that the right conferred by that subsection—

(a) is exercisable only along specified routes or ways,

(b) is exercisable only after entering the land at a specified place or places,

(c) is exercisable only by persons who do not take dogs on the land, or

(d) is exercisable only by persons who satisfy any other specified conditions.

(4) In this Chapter, except section 23(1), "owner", in relation to land which is subject to a farm business tenancy within the meaning of the Agricultural Tenancies Act 1995 or a tenancy to which the Agricultural Holdings Act 1986 applies, means the tenant under that tenancy.

1995 c. 8.
1986 c. 5.

(5) Subject to subsection (6), in this Chapter "the relevant authority"—

(a) in relation to any land in a National Park, means the National Park authority, and

(b) in relation to any other land, means the appropriate countryside body.

(6) Where—

(a) it appears to the Forestry Commissioners that any land which is dedicated for the purposes of this Part under section 16 consists wholly or predominantly of woodland, and

(b) the Forestry Commissioners give to the body who are apart from this subsection the relevant authority for the purposes of this Chapter in relation to the land a notice stating that the Forestry Commissioners are to be the relevant authority for those purposes as from a date specified in the notice,

the Forestry Commissioners shall as from that date become the relevant authority in relation to that land for those purposes, but subject to subsection (7).

(7) Where it appears to the Forestry Commissioners that any land in relation to which they are by virtue of subsection (6) the relevant authority for the purposes of this Chapter has ceased to consist wholly or predominantly of woodland, the Forestry Commissioners may, by giving notice to the body who would apart from subsection (6) be the relevant authority, revoke the notice under subsection (6) as from a date specified in the notice under this subsection.

Exclusion or restriction at discretion of owner and others.

22.—(1) Subject to subsections (2) and (6), an entitled person may, by giving notice to the relevant authority in accordance with regulations under section 32(1)(a), exclude or restrict access by virtue of section 2(1) to any land on one or more days specified in the notice.

(2) The number of days on which any entitled person excludes or restricts under this section access by virtue of section 2(1) to any land must not in any calendar year exceed the relevant maximum.

(3) In this section "entitled person", in relation to any land, means—

(a) the owner of the land, and

(b) any other person having an interest in the land and falling within a prescribed description.

(4) Subject to subsection (5), in this section "the relevant maximum" means twenty-eight.

(5) If regulations are made under subsection (3)(b), the regulations must provide that, in cases where there are two or more entitled persons having different interests in the land, the relevant maximum in relation to each of them is to be determined in accordance with the regulations, but so that the number of days on which access by virtue of section 2(1) to any land may be excluded or restricted under this section in any calendar year does not exceed twenty-eight.

(6) An entitled person may not under this section exclude or restrict access by virtue of section 2(1) to any land on—

(a) Christmas Day or Good Friday, or

(b) any day which is a bank holiday under the Banking and Financial Dealings Act 1971 in England and Wales. 1971 c. 80.

(7) An entitled person may not under this section exclude or restrict access by virtue of section 2(1) to any land—

(a) on more than four days in any calendar year which are either Saturday or Sunday,

(b) on any Saturday in the period beginning with 1st June and ending with 11th August in any year,

(c) on any Sunday in the period beginning with 1st June and ending with 30th September in any year.

(8) Regulations may provide that any exclusion or restriction under subsection (1) of access by virtue of section 2(1) to any land must relate to an area of land the boundaries of which are determined in accordance with the regulations.

23.—(1) The owner of any land consisting of moor managed for the breeding and shooting of grouse may, so far as appears to him to be necessary in connection with the management of the land for that purpose, by taking such steps as may be prescribed, provide that, during a specified period, the right conferred by section 2(1) is exercisable only by persons who do not take dogs on the land. Restrictions on dogs at discretion of owner.

(2) The owner of any land may, so far as appears to him to be necessary in connection with lambing, by taking such steps as may be prescribed, provide that during a specified period the right conferred by section 2(1) is exercisable only by persons who do not take dogs into any field or enclosure on the land in which there are sheep.

(3) In subsection (2) "field or enclosure" means a field or enclosure of not more than 15 hectares.

(4) As respects any land—

(a) any period specified under subsection (1) may not be more than five years,

(b) not more than one period may be specified under subsection (2) in any calendar year, and that period may not be more than six weeks.

(5) A restriction imposed under subsection (1) or (2) does not prevent a blind person from taking with him a trained guide dog, or a deaf person from taking with him a trained hearing dog.

Land
management.

24.—(1) The relevant authority may by direction, on an application made by a person interested in any land, exclude or restrict access to that land by virtue of section 2(1) during a specified period, if the authority are satisfied that the exclusion or restriction under this section of access by virtue of section 2(1) to the extent provided by the direction is necessary for the purposes of the management of the land by the applicant.

(2) The reference in subsection (1) to a specified period includes a reference to—

    (a) a specified period in every calendar year, or

    (b) a period which is to be—

        (i) determined by the applicant in accordance with the direction, and

        (ii) notified by him to the relevant authority in accordance with regulations under section 32(1)(d).

(3) In determining whether to any extent the exclusion or restriction under this section of access by virtue of section 2(1) during any period is necessary for the purposes of land management, the relevant authority shall have regard to—

    (a) the existence of the right conferred by section 22,

    (b) the extent to which the applicant has exercised or proposes to exercise that right, and

    (c) the purposes for which he has exercised or proposes to exercise it.

(4) Where an application under this section relates to land which is not access land at the time when the application is made, the relevant authority shall not give a direction under this section unless they are satisfied that it is likely that the land will be access land during all or part of the period to which the application relates.

Avoidance of risk
of fire or of
danger to the
public.

25.—(1) The relevant authority may by direction exclude or restrict access by virtue of section 2(1) in relation to any land during a specified period if the authority are satisfied—

    (a) that, by reason of any exceptional conditions of weather or any exceptional change in the condition of the land, the exclusion or restriction under this section of access to the land by virtue of section 2(1) to the extent provided by the direction is necessary for the purpose of fire prevention, or

    (b) that, by reason of anything done, or proposed to be done, on the land or on adjacent land, the exclusion or restriction under this section of access to the land by virtue of section 2(1) to the extent provided by the direction is necessary for the purpose of avoiding danger to the public.

(2) The reference in subsection (1) to a specified period includes a reference to—

    (a) a specified period in every calendar year, and

(b) a period which is to be—

    (i) determined by a specified person in accordance with the direction, and

    (ii) notified by him to the relevant authority in accordance with regulations under section 32(1)(d).

(3) The relevant authority may exercise their powers under subsection (1) on the application of any person interested in the land, or without any such application having been made.

(4) In determining on an application made by a person interested in the land whether the condition in subsection (1)(a) or (b) is satisfied, the relevant authority shall have regard to—

(a) the existence of the right conferred by section 22,

(b) the extent to which the applicant has exercised or proposes to exercise that right, and

(c) the purposes for which he has exercised or proposes to exercise it.

(5) Where an application under this section relates to land which is not access land at the time when the application is made, the relevant authority shall not give a direction under this section unless they are satisfied that it is likely that the land will be access land during all or part of the period to which the application relates.

26.—(1) The relevant authority may by direction exclude or restrict access by virtue of section 2(1) to any land during any period if they are satisfied that the exclusion or restriction of access by virtue of section 2(1) to the extent provided by the direction is necessary for either of the purposes specified in subsection (3).

Nature conservation and heritage preservation.

(2) A direction under subsection (1) may be expressed to have effect—

(a) during a period specified in the direction,

(b) during a specified period in every calendar year, or

(c) during a period which is to be—

    (i) determined by a specified person in accordance with the direction, and

    (ii) notified by him to the relevant authority in accordance with regulations under section 32(1)(d), or

(d) indefinitely.

(3) The purposes referred to in subsection (1) are—

(a) the purpose of conserving flora, fauna or geological or physiographical features of the land in question;

(b) the purpose of preserving—

    (i) any scheduled monument as defined by section 1(11) of the Ancient Monuments and Archaeological Areas Act 1979, or

1979 c. 46.

    (ii) any other structure, work, site, garden or area which is of historic, architectural, traditional, artistic or archaeological interest.

(4) In considering whether to give a direction under this section, the relevant authority shall have regard to any advice given to them by the relevant advisory body.

(5) Subsection (4) does not apply where the direction is given by the Countryside Council for Wales for the purpose specified in subsection (3)(a) or revokes a direction given by them for that purpose.

(6) In this section "the relevant advisory body"—

(a) in relation to a direction which is to be given for the purpose specified in subsection (3)(a) or which revokes a direction given for that purpose, means—

(i) in the case of land in England, English Nature, and

(ii) in the case of land in Wales in respect of which the Countryside Council for Wales are not the relevant authority, the Countryside Council for Wales, and

(b) in relation to a direction which is to be given for the purpose specified in subsection (3)(b) or which revokes a direction given for that purpose, means—

(i) in the case of land in England, the Historic Buildings and Monuments Commission for England, and

(ii) in the case of land in Wales, the National Assembly for Wales.

Directions by relevant authority: general.

27.—(1) Before giving a direction under section 24, 25 or 26 in relation to land in an area for which there is a local access forum so as to exclude or restrict access to the land—

(a) indefinitely, or

(b) during a period which exceeds, or may exceed, six months,

the relevant authority shall consult the local access forum.

(2) Any direction under section 24, 25 or 26 may be revoked or varied by a subsequent direction under that provision.

(3) Where a direction given under section 24, 25 or 26 in relation to any land by the relevant authority excludes or restricts access to the land—

(a) indefinitely,

(b) for part of every year or of each of six or more consecutive calendar years, or

(c) for a specified period of more than five years,

the authority shall review the direction not later than the fifth anniversary of the relevant date.

(4) In subsection (3) "the relevant date", in relation to a direction, means—

(a) the day on which the direction was given, or

(b) where it has already been reviewed, the day on which it was last reviewed.

(5) Before revoking or varying a direction under section 24 or 25 which was given on the application of a person interested in the land to which the direction relates ("the original applicant"), the relevant authority shall—

(a) where the original applicant still holds the interest in the land which he held when he applied for the direction and it is reasonably practicable to consult him, consult the original applicant, and

(b) where the original applicant does not hold that interest, consult any person who holds that interest and with whom consultation is reasonably practicable.

(6) Before revoking or varying a direction under section 26, the relevant authority shall consult the relevant advisory body as defined by section 26(6), unless the direction falls within section 26(5).

28.—(1) The Secretary of State may by direction exclude or restrict access by virtue of section 2(1) to any land during any period if he is satisfied that the exclusion or restriction of such access to the extent provided by the direction is necessary for the purposes of defence or national security.

Defence or national security.

(2) A direction under subsection (1) may be expressed to have effect—

(a) during a period specified in the direction,

(b) during a specified period in every calendar year,

(c) during a period which is to be—

(i) determined in accordance with the direction by a person authorised by the Secretary of State, and

(ii) notified by that person to the relevant authority in accordance with regulations under section 32(1)(c), or

(d) indefinitely.

(3) Any direction given by the Secretary of State under this section may be revoked or varied by a subsequent direction.

(4) Where a direction given under this section in relation to any land excludes or restricts access to the land—

(a) indefinitely,

(b) for part of every year or of each of six or more consecutive calendar years, or

(c) for a specified period of more than five years,

the Secretary of State shall review the direction not later than the fifth anniversary of the relevant date.

(5) In subsection (4) "the relevant date", in relation to a direction, means—

(a) the day on which the direction was given, or

(b) where it has previously been reviewed, the day on which it was last reviewed.

(6) If in any calendar year the Secretary of State reviews a defence direction, he shall—

(a) prepare a report on all reviews of defence directions which he has undertaken during that year, and

(b) lay a copy of the report before each House of Parliament.

(7) In subsection (6) "defence direction" means a direction given under this section for the purposes of defence.

29.—(1) Subsections (2) and (3) apply where—

(a) the relevant advisory body has given advice under section 26(4) or on being consulted under section 27(6), but

Reference by relevant advisory body.

(b) in any respect, the relevant authority decide not to act in accordance with that advice.

(2) The relevant advisory body may refer the decision—

(a) in the case of land in England, to the appropriate Minister, or

(b) in the case of land in Wales, to the National Assembly for Wales.

(3) On a reference under this section the appropriate Minister or the National Assembly for Wales may, if he or it thinks fit—

(a) cancel any direction given by the relevant authority, or

(b) require the relevant authority to give such direction under section 26 as the appropriate Minister or, as the case may be, the Assembly, think fit.

(4) Sections 7 and 8 (and Schedule 3) have effect in relation to a reference under this section as they have effect in relation to an appeal under section 6 but as if references to the Secretary of State were references to the appropriate Minister.

(5) In this section—

"the appropriate Minister" means—

(a) in relation to land as respects which by virtue of section 21(6) the Forestry Commissioners are the relevant authority, the Minister of Agriculture, Fisheries and Food, and

(b) in relation to other land, the Secretary of State;

"the relevant advisory body" has the same meaning as in section 26, except that it does not include the National Assembly for Wales.

Appeal by person
interested in land.

30.—(1) Subsections (2) and (3) apply where—

(a) a person interested in any land (in this section referred to as "the applicant")—

(i) has applied for a direction under section 24 or 25, or

(ii) has made representations on being consulted under section 27(5), but

(b) in any respect, the relevant authority decide not to act in accordance with the application or the representations.

(2) The relevant authority shall inform the applicant of their reasons for not acting in accordance with the application or representations.

(3) The applicant may appeal against the decision—

(a) in the case of land in England, to the appropriate Minister, or

(b) in the case of land in Wales, to the National Assembly for Wales.

(4) On appeal under this section the appropriate Minister or the National Assembly for Wales may, if he or it thinks fit—

(a) cancel any direction given by the relevant authority, or

(b) require the relevant authority to give such direction under section 24 or 25 as the appropriate Minister or, as the case may be, the Assembly, think fit.

(5) Sections 7 and 8 (and Schedule 3) have effect in relation to an appeal under this section as they have effect in relation to an appeal under section 6 but as if references to the Secretary of State were references to the appropriate Minister.

(6) In this section "the appropriate Minister" has the same meaning as in section 29.

31.—(1) Regulations may make provision enabling the relevant authority, where the authority are satisfied that an emergency has arisen which makes the exclusion or restriction of access by virtue of section 2(1) necessary for any of the purposes specified in section 24(1), 25(1) or 26(3), by direction to exclude or restrict such access in respect of any land for a period not exceeding three months.

(2) Regulations under this section may provide for any of the preceding provisions of this Chapter to apply in relation to a direction given under the regulations with such modifications as may be prescribed.

32.—(1) Regulations may make provision—

(a) as to the giving of notice under section 22(1),

(b) as to the steps to be taken under section 23(1) and (2),

(c) as to the procedure on any application to the relevant authority under section 24 or 25, including the period within which any such application must be made,

(d) as to the giving of notice for the purposes of section 24(2)(b)(ii), 25(2)(b)(ii), 26(2)(c)(ii) or 28(2)(c)(ii),

(e) prescribing the form of any notice or application referred to in paragraphs (a) to (d),

(f) restricting the cases in which a person who is interested in any land only as the holder of rights of common may make an application under section 24 or 25 in respect of the land,

(g) as to requirements to be met by relevant authorities or the Secretary of State in relation to consultation (whether or not required by the preceding provisions of this Chapter),

(h) as to the giving of directions by relevant authorities or the Secretary of State,

(i) as to notification by relevant authorities or the Secretary of State of decisions under this Chapter,

(j) as to steps to be taken by persons interested in land, by relevant authorities, by the bodies specified in section 26(6) or by the Secretary of State for informing the public about the exclusion or restriction under this Chapter of access by virtue of section 2(1), including the display of notices on or near the land to which the exclusion or restriction relates,

(k) as to the carrying out of reviews by relevant authorities under section 27(3) or by the Secretary of State under section 28(4),

(l) as to the period within which and manner in which appeals under section 30 are to be brought,

(m) as to the advertising of such an appeal, and

(n) as to the manner in which such appeals are to be considered.

(2) Regulations made under subsection (1)(k) may provide for any of the provisions of this Chapter relating to appeals to apply (with or without modifications) on a review under section 27.

Guidance by
countryside bodies
to National Park
authorities.

33.—(1) Subject to subsection (3), the Countryside Agency may issue guidance—

(a) to National Park authorities in England with respect to the discharge by National Park authorities of their functions under this Chapter, and

(b) to the Forestry Commissioners with respect to the discharge by the Forestry Commissioners of any functions conferred on them by virtue of section 21(6) in relation to land in England.

(2) Subject to subsection (3), the Countryside Council for Wales may issue guidance—

(a) to National Park authorities in Wales with respect to the discharge by National Park authorities of their functions under this Chapter, and

(b) to the Forestry Commissioners with respect to the discharge by the Forestry Commissioners of any functions conferred on them by virtue of section 21(6) in relation to land in Wales.

(3) The Countryside Agency or the Countryside Council for Wales may not issue any guidance under this section unless the guidance has been approved—

(a) in the case of the Countryside Agency, by the Secretary of State, and

(b) in the case of the Countryside Council for Wales, by the National Assembly for Wales.

(4) Where the Countryside Agency or the Countryside Council for Wales issue any guidance under this section, they shall arrange for the guidance to be published in such manner as they consider appropriate.

(5) A National Park authority or the Forestry Commissioners shall have regard to any guidance issued to them under this section.

CHAPTER III

MEANS OF ACCESS

Interpretation of
Chapter III.

34. In this Chapter—

"access land" does not include any land in relation to which the application of section 2(1) has been excluded under any provision of Chapter II either indefinitely or for a specified period of which at least six months remain unexpired;

"means of access", in relation to land, means—

(a) any opening in a wall, fence or hedge bounding the land (or part of the land), with or without a gate, stile or other works for regulating passage through the opening,

(b) any stairs or steps for enabling persons to enter on the land (or part of the land), or

(c) any bridge, stepping stone or other works for crossing a watercourse, ditch or bog on the land or adjoining the boundary of the land.

35.—(1) Where, in respect of any access land, it appears to the access authority that—

Agreements with respect to means of access.

(a) the opening-up, improvement or repair of any means of access to the land,

(b) the construction of any new means of access to the land,

(c) the maintenance of any means of access to the land, or

(d) the imposition of restrictions—

(i) on the destruction, removal, alteration or stopping-up of any means of access to the land, or

(ii) on the doing of any thing whereby the use of any such means of access to the land by the public would be impeded,

is necessary for giving the public reasonable access to that land in exercise of the right conferred by section 2(1), the access authority may enter into an agreement with the owner or occupier of the land as to the carrying out of the works or the imposition of the restrictions.

(2) An agreement under this section may provide—

(a) for the carrying out of works by the owner or occupier or by the access authority, and

(b) for the making of payments by the access authority—

(i) as a contribution towards, or for the purpose of defraying, costs incurred by the owner or occupier in carrying out any works for which the agreement provides, or

(ii) in consideration of the imposition of any restriction.

36.—(1) If the owner or occupier of any access land fails to carry out within the required time any works which he is required by an agreement under section 35 to carry out, the access authority, after giving not less than twenty-one days' notice of their intention to do so, may take all necessary steps for carrying out those works.

Failure to comply with agreement.

(2) In subsection (1) "the required time" means the time specified in, or determined in accordance with, the agreement as that within which the works must be carried out or, if there is no such time, means a reasonable time.

(3) If the owner or occupier of any access land fails to observe any restriction which he is required by an agreement under section 35 to observe, the access authority may give him a notice requiring him within a specified period of not less than twenty-one days to carry out such works as may be specified in the notice, for the purpose of remedying the failure to observe the restriction.

(4) A notice under subsection (3) must contain particulars of the right of appeal conferred by section 38.

(5) If the person to whom a notice under subsection (3) is given fails to comply with the notice, the access authority may take all necessary steps for carrying out any works specified in the notice.

(6) Where the access authority carry out any works by virtue of subsection (1), the authority may recover the amount of any expenses reasonably incurred by them in carrying out the works, reduced by their

contribution under the agreement, from the person by whom under the agreement the cost (apart from the authority's contribution) of carrying out the works would fall to be borne.

(7) Where the access authority carry out any works by virtue of subsection (5), the authority may recover the amount of any expenses reasonably incurred by them in carrying out the works from the person to whom the notice under subsection (3) was given.

Provision of access by access authority in absence of agreement.

37.—(1) Where, in respect of any access land—

   (a) it appears to the access authority that—

      (i) the opening-up, improvement or repair of any means of access to the land,

      (ii) the construction of any new means of access to the land, or

      (iii) the maintenance of any means of access to the land,

     is necessary for giving the public reasonable access to that land, or to other access land, in pursuance of the right conferred by section 2(1), and

   (b) the access authority are satisfied that they are unable to conclude on reasonable terms an agreement under section 35 with the owner or occupier of the land for the carrying out of the works,

the access authority may, subject to subsection (3), give the owner or occupier a notice stating that, after the end of a specified period of not less than twenty-one days, the authority intend to take all necessary steps for carrying out the works specified in the notice for the opening-up, improvement, repair, construction or maintenance of the means of access.

(2) A notice under subsection (1) must contain particulars of the right of appeal conferred by section 38.

(3) Where a notice under subsection (1) is given to any person as the owner or occupier of any land, the access authority shall give a copy of the notice to every other owner or occupier of the land.

(4) An access authority exercising the power conferred by subsection (1) in relation to the provision of a means of access shall have regard to the requirements of efficient management of the land in deciding where the means of access is to be provided.

(5) If, at the end of the period specified in a notice under subsection (1), any of the works specified in the notice have not been carried out, the access authority may take all necessary steps for carrying out those works.

Appeals relating to notices.

38.—(1) Where a notice under section 36(3) or 37(1) has been given to a person in respect of any land, he or any other owner or occupier of the land may appeal against the notice—

   (a) in the case of land in England, to the Secretary of State, and

   (b) in the case of land in Wales, to the National Assembly for Wales.

(2) An appeal against a notice under section 36(3) may be brought on any of the following grounds—

   (a) that the notice requires the carrying out of any works which are not necessary for remedying a breach of the agreement,

   (b) that any of the works have already been carried out, and

(c) that the period specified in the notice as that before the end of which the works must be carried out is too short.

(3) An appeal against a notice under section 37(1) may be brought on any of the following grounds—

(a) that the notice requires the carrying out of any works which are not necessary for giving the public reasonable access to the access land in question,

(b) in the case of works to provide a means of access, that the means of access should be provided elsewhere, or that a different means of access should be provided, and

(c) that any of the works have already been carried out.

(4) On an appeal under this section, the Secretary of State or the National Assembly for Wales may—

(a) confirm the notice with or without modifications, or

(b) cancel the notice.

(5) Sections 7 and 8 (and Schedule 3) have effect in relation to an appeal under this section as they have effect in relation to an appeal under section 6.

(6) Regulations may make provision as to—

(a) the period within which and manner in which appeals under this section are to be brought,

(b) the advertising of such an appeal, and

(c) the manner in which such appeals are to be considered.

(7) Where an appeal has been brought under this section against a notice under section 36(3) or 37(1), the access authority may not exercise their powers under section 36(5) or section 37(5) (as the case may be) pending the determination or withdrawal of the appeal.

39.—(1) Where at any time two or more access notices relating to a means of access have been given to any person within the preceding thirty-six months, a magistrates' court may, on the application of the access authority, order that person—

Order to remove obstruction.

(a) within such time as may be specified in the order, to take such steps as may be so specified to remove any obstruction of that means of access, and

(b) not to obstruct that means of access at any time when the right conferred by section 2(1) is exercisable.

(2) If a person ("the person in default") fails to comply with an order under this section—

(a) he is liable on summary conviction to a fine not exceeding level 3 on the standard scale, and

(b) the access authority may remove any obstruction of the means of access and recover from the person in default the costs reasonably incurred by them in doing so.

(3) In this section "access notice" means a notice under section 36(3) or 37(1) in respect of which the period specified in the notice has expired, other than a notice in respect of which an appeal is pending or which has been cancelled on appeal.

CHAPTER IV

GENERAL

Powers of entry
for purposes of
Part I.

40.—(1) A person who is authorised by the appropriate countryside body to do so may enter any land—

(a) for the purpose of surveying it in connection with the preparation of any map under this Part or the review of any map issued under this Part,

(b) for the purpose of determining whether any power conferred on the appropriate countryside body by Chapter II should be exercised in relation to the land,

(c) for the purpose of ascertaining whether members of the public are being permitted to exercise the right conferred by section 2(1),

(d) in connection with an appeal under any provision of this Part, or

(e) for the purpose of determining whether to apply to the Secretary of State or the National Assembly for Wales under section 58.

(2) A person who is authorised by a local highway authority to do so may enter any land—

(a) for the purpose of determining whether the local highway authority should enter into an agreement under section 35, give a notice under section 36(1) or (3) or section 37(1) or carry out works under section 36(1) or (5), section 37(5) or section 39(2)(b),

(b) for the purpose of ascertaining whether an offence under section 14 or 39 has been or is being committed, or

(c) for the purposes of erecting or maintaining notices under section 19(1).

(3) A person who is authorised by a National Park authority to do so may enter any land—

(a) for the purpose of enabling the authority to determine whether to exercise any power under Chapter II of this Act in relation to the land,

(b) for the purpose of determining whether members of the public are being permitted to exercise the right conferred by section 2(1),

(c) in connection with an appeal under any provision of this Part,

(d) for the purpose of determining whether the authority should enter into an agreement under section 35, give a notice under section 36(1) or (3) or section 37(1) or carry out works under section 36(1) or (5), section 37(5) or section 39(2)(b),

(e) for the purpose of ascertaining whether an offence under section 14 or 39 has been or is being committed, or

(f) for the purposes of erecting or maintaining notices under section 19(1).

(4) A person who is authorised by the Forestry Commissioners to do so may enter any land—

(a) for the purpose of determining whether any power conferred on the Forestry Commissioners by Chapter II should be exercised in relation to the land, or

(b) in connection with an appeal under any provision of this Part.

(5) A person acting in the exercise of a power conferred by this section may—

    (a) use a vehicle to enter the land;

    (b) take a constable with him if he reasonably believes he is likely to be obstructed;

    (c) take with him equipment and materials needed for the purpose for which he is exercising the power of entry;

    (d) take samples of the land and of anything on it.

(6) If in the exercise of a power conferred by this section a person enters land which is unoccupied or from which the occupier is temporarily absent, he must on his departure leave it as effectively secured against unauthorised entry as he found it.

(7) A person authorised under this section to enter upon any land—

    (a) shall, if so required, produce evidence of his authority before entering, and

    (b) shall produce such evidence if required to do so at any time while he remains on the land.

(8) A person shall not under this section demand admission as of right to any occupied land, other than access land, unless—

    (a) at least twenty-four hours' notice of the intended entry has been given to the occupier, or

    (b) it is not reasonably practicable to give such notice, or

    (c) the entry is for the purpose specified in subsection (2)(b) and (3)(e).

(9) The rights conferred by this section are not exercisable in relation to a dwelling.

(10) A person who intentionally obstructs a person acting in the exercise of his powers under this section is guilty of an offence and liable on summary conviction to a fine not exceeding level 2 on the standard scale.

41.—(1) It is the duty of a body by which an authorisation may be given under section 40 to compensate any person who has sustained damage as a result of—

Compensation relating to powers under s. 40.

    (a) the exercise of a power conferred by that section by a person authorised by that body to do so, or

    (b) the failure of a person so authorised to perform the duty imposed on him by subsection (6) of that section,

except where the damage is attributable to the fault of the person who sustained it.

(2) Any dispute as to a person's entitlement to compensation under this section or as to its amount shall be referred to an arbitrator to be appointed, in default of agreement—

    (a) as respects entry on land in England, by the Secretary of State, and

(b) as respects entry on land in Wales, by the National Assembly for Wales.

References to
public places in
existing
enactments.

42.—(1) This section applies to any enactment which—

(a) is contained in an Act passed before or in the same Session as this Act, and

(b) relates to things done, or omitted to be done, in public places or places to which the public have access.

(2) Regulations may provide that, in determining for the purposes of any specified enactment to which this section applies whether a place is a public place or a place to which the public have access, the right conferred by section 2(1), or access by virtue of that right, is to be disregarded, either generally or in prescribed cases.

Crown application
of Part I.

43.—(1) This Part binds the Crown.

(2) No contravention by the Crown of any provision of this Part shall make the Crown criminally liable; but the High Court may declare unlawful any act or omission of the Crown which constitutes such a contravention.

(3) The provisions of this Part apply to persons in the public service of the Crown as they apply to other persons.

Orders and
regulations under
Part I.

44.—(1) Any power to make an order or regulations which is conferred by this Part on the Secretary of State or the National Assembly for Wales is exercisable by statutory instrument.

(2) Any power to make an order or regulations which is conferred by this Part on the Secretary of State or the National Assembly for Wales includes power—

(a) to make different provision for different cases, and

(b) to make such incidental, supplementary, consequential or transitional provision as the person making the order or regulations considers necessary or expedient.

(3) No order under section 3 or regulations under paragraph 3 of Schedule 2 shall be made by the Secretary of State unless a draft has been laid before, and approved by a resolution of, each House of Parliament.

(4) Any statutory instrument containing regulations made by the Secretary of State under any other provision of this Part shall be subject to annulment in pursuance of a resolution of either House of Parliament.

Interpretation of
Part I.

45.—(1) In this Part, unless a contrary intention appears—

"access authority" has the meaning given by section 1(2);

"access land" has the meaning given by section 1(1);

"the appropriate countryside body" has the meaning given by section 1(2);

"excepted land" has the meaning given by section 1(2);

"Inner London" means the area comprising the inner London boroughs, the City of London, the Inner Temple and the Middle Temple;

"interest", in relation to land, includes any estate in land and any right over land, whether the right is exercisable by virtue of the ownership of an estate or interest in land or by virtue of a licence or agreement, and in particular includes rights of common and sporting rights, and references to a person interested in land shall be construed accordingly;

"livestock" means cattle, sheep, goats, swine, horses or poultry, and for the purposes of this definition "cattle" means bulls, cows, oxen, heifers or calves, "horses" include asses and mules, and "poultry" means domestic fowls, turkeys, geese or ducks;

"local highway authority" has the same meaning as in the Highways Act 1980;   *1980 c. 66.*

"local or private Act" includes an Act confirming a provisional order;

"mountain" has the meaning given by section 1(2);

"open country" has the meaning given by section 1(2);

"owner", in relation to any land, means, subject to subsection (2), any person, other than a mortgagee not in possession, who, whether in his own right or as trustee for another person, is entitled to receive the rack rent of the land, or, where the land is not let at a rack rent, would be so entitled if it were so let;

"prescribed" means prescribed by regulations;

"registered common land" has the meaning given by section 1(3);

"regulations" means regulations made by the Secretary of State (as respects England) or by the National Assembly for Wales (as respects Wales);

"rights of common" has the same meaning as in the Commons Registration Act 1965;   *1965 c. 64.*

"telecommunications code" and "telecommunications code system" have the same meaning as in Schedule 4 to the Telecommunications Act 1984.   *1984 c. 12.*

(2) In relation to any land which is subject to a farm business tenancy within the meaning of the Agricultural Tenancies Act 1995 or a tenancy to which the Agricultural Holdings Act 1986 applies, the definition of "owner" in subsection (1) does not apply where it is excluded by section 2(5) or 21(4) or by paragraph 7(4) of Schedule 2.   *1995 c. 8.*   *1986 c. 5.*

(3) For the purposes of this Part, the Broads are to be treated as a National Park and the Broads Authority as a National Park authority.

(4) In subsection (3) "the Broads" has the same meaning as in the Norfolk and Suffolk Broads Act 1988.   *1988 c. 4.*

46.—(1) The following provisions (which are superseded by the provisions of this Part) shall cease to have effect—   Repeal of previous legislation, and amendments relating to Part I.

  (a) in section 193 of the Law of Property Act 1925, subsection (2) (power by deed to declare land subject to that section), and   *1925 c. 20.*

  (b) sections 61 to 63 of the National Parks and Access to the Countryside Act 1949 (which relate to reviews of access requirements and the preparation of maps).   *1949 c. 97.*

1949 c. 97.

(2) No access agreement or access order under Part V of the National Parks and Access to the Countryside Act 1949 (access to open country) may be made after the commencement of this section in relation to land which is open country or registered common land for the purposes of this Part.

(3) Schedule 4 (which contains minor and consequential amendments relating to access to the countryside) has effect.

PART II

PUBLIC RIGHTS OF WAY AND ROAD TRAFFIC

Public rights of way and definitive maps and statements

Redesignation of roads used as public paths.
1981 c. 69.

47.—(1) In the Wildlife and Countryside Act 1981 (in this Act referred to as "the 1981 Act"), section 54 (duty to reclassify roads used as public paths) shall cease to have effect.

(2) Every way which, immediately before the commencement of this section, is shown in any definitive map and statement as a road used as a public path shall be treated instead as shown as a restricted byway; and the expression "road used as a public path" shall not be used in any definitive map and statement to describe any way.

Restricted byway rights.

48.—(1) Subject to subsections (2) and (3), the public shall have restricted byway rights over any way which, immediately before the commencement of section 47, is shown in a definitive map and statement as a road used as a public path.

(2) Subsection (1) has effect subject to the operation of any enactment or instrument (whether coming into operation before or after the commencement of section 47), and to the effect of any event otherwise within section 53(3)(a) of the 1981 Act, whereby a highway—

(a) is authorised to be stopped up, diverted, widened or extended, or

(b) becomes a public path;

and subsection (1) applies accordingly to any way as so diverted, widened or extended.

(3) Subsection (1) does not apply to any way, or part of a way, over which immediately before the commencement of section 47 there was no public right of way.

(4) In this Part—

"restricted byway rights" means—

(a) a right of way on foot,

(b) a right of way on horseback or leading a horse, and

(c) a right of way for vehicles other than mechanically propelled vehicles; and

"restricted byway" means a highway over which the public have restricted byway rights, with or without a right to drive animals of any description along the highway, but no other rights of way.

(5) A highway at the side of a river, canal or other inland navigation is not excluded from the definition of "restricted byway" in subsection (4)

merely because the public have a right to use the highway for purposes of navigation, if the highway would fall within that definition if the public had no such right over it.

(6) Subsection (1) is without prejudice to any question whether the public have over any way, in addition to restricted byway rights, a right of way for mechanically propelled vehicles or any other right.

(7) In subsections (4) and (6) "mechanically propelled vehicle" does not include a vehicle falling within paragraph (c) of section 189(1) of the Road Traffic Act 1988.

1988 c. 52.

(8) Every surveying authority shall take such steps as they consider expedient for bringing to the attention of the public the effect of section 47(2) and this section.

(9) The powers conferred by section 103(5) must be so exercised as to secure that nothing in section 47 or this section affects the operation of section 53 or 54 of, or Schedule 14 or 15 to, the 1981 Act in relation to—

    (a) a relevant order made before the commencement of section 47, or

    (b) an application made before that commencement for a relevant order.

(10) In subsection (9) "relevant order" means an order which relates to a way shown in a definitive map and statement as a road used as a public path and which—

    (a) is made under section 53 of the 1981 Act and contains modifications relating to that way by virtue of subsection (3)(c)(ii) of that section, or

    (b) is made under section 54 of the 1981 Act.

(11) Where—

    (a) by virtue of an order under subsection (3) of section 103 ("the commencement order") containing such provision as is mentioned in subsection (5) of that section, an order under Part III of the 1981 Act ("the Part III order") takes effect, after the commencement of section 47, in relation to any way which, immediately before that commencement, was shown in a definitive map and statement as a road used as a public path,

    (b) the commencement order does not prevent subsection (1) from having effect on that commencement in relation to that way, and

    (c) if the Part III order had taken effect before that commencement, that way would not have fallen within subsection (1),

all rights over that way which exist only by virtue of subsection (1) shall be extinguished when the Part III order takes effect.

49.—(1) Every way over which the public have restricted byway rights by virtue of subsection (1) of section 48 (whether or not they also have a right of way for mechanically propelled vehicles or any other right) shall, as from the commencement of that section, be a highway maintainable at the public expense.

Provisions supplementary to ss. 47 and 48.

1980 c. 66.

(2) As from the commencement of that section, any liability, under a special enactment (within the meaning of the Highways Act 1980) or by reason of tenure, enclosure or prescription, to maintain, otherwise than as a highway maintainable at the public expense, a restricted byway to which subsection (1) applies is extinguished.

(3) Every way which, in pursuance of—

1968 c. 41.

 (a) paragraph 9 of Part III of Schedule 3 to the Countryside Act 1968, or

 (b) any order made under section 54(1) of the 1981 Act before the coming into force of section 47,

is shown in any definitive map and statement as a byway open to all traffic, a bridleway or a footpath, shall continue to be maintainable at the public expense.

(4) Nothing in subsections (1) and (3) or in section 48(1) obliges a highway authority to provide on any way a metalled carriage-way or a carriage-way which is by any other means provided with a surface suitable for cycles or other vehicles.

1984 c. 27.

(5) Nothing in section 48, or in section 53 of the 1981 Act, limits the operation of orders under the Road Traffic Regulation Act 1984 or the operation of any byelaws.

(6) Section 67 of the 1981 Act (application to the Crown) has effect as if this section and sections 47, 48 and 50 were contained in Part III of that Act.

Private rights over restricted byways.

50.—(1) Restricted byway rights over any way by virtue of subsection (1) of section 48 are subject to any condition or limitation to which public rights of way over that way were subject immediately before the commencement of that section.

(2) Any owner or lessee of premises adjoining or adjacent to a relevant highway shall, so far as is necessary for the reasonable enjoyment and occupation of the premises, have a right of way for vehicular and all other kinds of traffic over the relevant highway.

(3) In subsection (2), in its application to the owner of any premises, "relevant highway" means so much of any highway maintainable at the public expense by virtue of section 49(1) as was, immediately before it became so maintainable, owned by the person who then owned the premises.

(4) In subsection (2), in its application to the lessee of any premises, "relevant highway" means so much of any highway maintainable at the public expense by virtue of section 49(1) as was, immediately before it became so maintainable, included in the lease on which the premises are held.

(5) In this section—

"lease" and "lessee" have the same meaning as in the 1980 Act;

"owner", in relation to any premises, means a person, other than a mortgagee not in possession, who is for the time being entitled to dispose of the fee simple of the premises, whether in possession or in reversion, and "owned" shall be construed accordingly; and

"premises" has the same meaning as in the 1980 Act.

PART II
Amendments
relating to
definitive maps
and statements
and restricted
byways.
Restricted
byways: power to
amend existing
legislation.

51. Schedule 5 to this Act (which contains amendments relating to definitive maps and statements and restricted byways) has effect.

52.—(1) The Secretary of State may by regulations—

    (a) provide for any relevant provision which relates—

        (i) to highways or highways of a particular description,

        (ii) to things done on or in connection with highways or highways of a particular description, or

        (iii) to the creation, stopping up or diversion of highways or highways of a particular description,

    not to apply, or to apply with or without modification, in relation to restricted byways or to ways shown in a definitive map and statement as restricted byways, and

    (b) make in any relevant provision such amendments, repeals or revocations as appear to him appropriate in consequence of the coming into force of sections 47 to 50 or provision made by virtue of paragraph (a) or subsection (6)(a).

(2) In this section—

    "relevant provision" means a provision contained—

        (a) in an Act passed before or in the same Session as this Act, or

        (b) in any subordinate legislation made before the passing of this Act;

    "relevant Welsh provision" means a provision contained—

        (a) in a local or private Act passed before or in the same Session as this Act and relating only to areas in Wales, or

        (b) in any subordinate legislation which was made before the passing of this Act and which the National Assembly for Wales has power to amend or revoke as respects Wales.

(3) In exercising the power to make regulations under subsection (1), the Secretary of State—

    (a) may not make provision which has effect in relation to Wales unless he has consulted the National Assembly for Wales, and

    (b) may not without the consent of the National Assembly for Wales make any provision which (otherwise than merely by virtue of the amendment or repeal of a provision contained in an Act) amends or revokes subordinate legislation made by the Assembly.

(4) The National Assembly for Wales may submit to the Secretary of State proposals for the exercise by the Secretary of State of the power conferred by subsection (1).

(5) The powers conferred by subsection (1) may be exercised in relation to a relevant provision even though the provision is amended or inserted by this Act.

(6) As respects Wales, the National Assembly for Wales may by regulations—

    (a) provide for any relevant Welsh provision which relates—

        (i) to highways or highways of a particular description,

(ii) to things done on or in connection with highways or highways of a particular description, or

(iii) to the creation, stopping up or diversion of highways or highways of a particular description,

not to apply, or to apply with or without modification, in relation to restricted byways or to ways shown in a definitive map and statement as restricted byways, and

(b) make in any relevant Welsh provision such amendments, repeals or revocations as appear to the Assembly appropriate in consequence of the coming into force of sections 47 to 50 or provision made by virtue of subsection (1)(a) or paragraph (a).

(7) Regulations under this section shall be made by statutory instrument, but no such regulations shall be made by the Secretary of State unless a draft of the instrument containing them has been laid before, and approved by a resolution of, each House of Parliament.

(8) Where the Secretary of State lays before Parliament the draft of an instrument containing regulations under subsection (1) in respect of which consultation with the National Assembly for Wales is required by subsection (3)(a), he shall also lay before each House of Parliament a document giving details of the consultation and setting out any representations received from the Assembly.

Extinguishment of unrecorded rights of way.

53.—(1) Subsection (2) applies to a highway if—

(a) it was on 1st January 1949 a footpath or a bridleway, is on the cut-off date (in either case) a footpath or a bridleway, and between those dates has not been a highway of any other description,

(b) it is not on the cut-off date shown in a definitive map and statement as a highway of any description, and

(c) it is not on the cut-off date an excepted highway, as defined by section 54(1).

(2) All public rights of way over a highway to which this subsection applies shall be extinguished immediately after the cut-off date.

(3) Where a public right of way created before 1949—

(a) falls within subsection (4) on the cut-off date, and

(b) is not on that date an excepted right of way, as defined by section 54(5),

that right of way shall be extinguished immediately after the cut-off date.

(4) A public right of way falls within this subsection if it is—

(a) a public right of way on horseback, leading a horse or for vehicles over a bridleway, restricted byway or byway open to all traffic which is shown in a definitive map and statement as a footpath;

(b) a right for the public to drive animals of any description along a bridleway, restricted byway or byway open to all traffic which is shown in a definitive map and statement as a footpath;

(c) a public right of way for vehicles over a restricted byway or byway open to all traffic which is shown in a definitive map and statement as a bridleway; or

(d) a public right of way for mechanically propelled vehicles over a byway open to all traffic which is shown in a definitive map and statement as a restricted byway.

(5) Where by virtue of subsection (3) a highway ceases to be a bridleway, the right of way created over it by section 30 of the Countryside Act 1968 (riding of pedal cycles on bridleways) is also extinguished.

1968 c. 41.

(6) In determining—

(a) for the purposes of subsection (1) whether any part of a highway was on 1st January 1949 a footpath or bridleway, or

(b) for the purposes of subsection (3) whether a public right of way over any part of a highway was created before 1st January 1949,

any diversion, widening or extension of the highway on or after that date (and not later than the cut-off date) is to be treated as having occurred before 1st January 1949.

(7) Where a way shown on the cut-off date in a definitive map and statement has at any time been diverted, widened or extended, it is to be treated for the purposes of subsections (1) to (5) as shown as so diverted, widened or extended, whether or not it is so shown.

(8) In this section—

"cut-off date" has the meaning given in section 56, and

"mechanically propelled vehicle" does not include a vehicle falling within paragraph (c) of section 189(1) of the Road Traffic Act 1988.

1988 c. 52.

54.—(1) A footpath or bridleway is an excepted highway for the purposes of section 53(1) if—

Excepted highways and rights of way.

(a) it is a footpath or bridleway which satisfies either of the conditions in subsections (2) and (3),

(b) it is, or is part of, a footpath or bridleway any part of which is in an area which, immediately before 1st April 1965, formed part of the administrative county of London,

(c) it is a footpath or bridleway—

(i) at the side of (whether or not contiguous with) a carriageway constituting or comprised in another highway, or

(ii) between two carriageways comprised in the same highway (whether or not the footpath or bridleway is contiguous with either carriageway),

(d) it is a footpath or bridleway of such other description as may be specified in regulations made (as respects England) by the Secretary of State or (as respects Wales) by the National Assembly for Wales, or

(e) it is a footpath or bridleway so specified.

(2) A footpath or bridleway ("the relevant highway") satisfies the first condition if—

(a) it became a footpath or bridleway on or after 1st January 1949 by the diversion, widening or extension of a footpath or, as the case may be, of a bridleway by virtue of an event within section 53(3)(a) of the 1981 Act,

(b) it became a footpath on or after 1st January 1949 by the stopping up of a bridleway,

(c) it was on 1st January 1949 a footpath and is on the cut-off date a bridleway,

(d) it is so much of a footpath or bridleway as on or after 1st January 1949 has been stopped up as respects part only of its width, or

(e) it is so much of a footpath or bridleway as passes over a bridge or through a tunnel,

and it communicates with a retained highway, either directly or by means of one or more footpaths or bridleways each of which forms part of the same highway as the relevant highway and each of which either falls within any of paragraphs (a) to (e) or satisfies the condition in subsection (3).

(3) A footpath or bridleway satisfies the second condition if—

(a) it extends from a footpath or bridleway ("the relevant highway") which—

(i) falls within any of paragraphs (a) to (e) of subsection (2), or

(ii) is an excepted highway by virtue of subsection (1)(c),

to, but not beyond, a retained highway, and

(b) it forms part of the same highway as the relevant highway.

(4) A retained highway for the purposes of subsections (2) and (3) is any highway over which, otherwise than by virtue of subsection (1)(a), section 53(2) does not extinguish rights of way.

(5) A public right of way is an excepted right of way for the purposes of section 53(3) if—

(a) it subsists over land over which there subsists on the cut-off date any public right of way created on or after 1st January 1949 otherwise than by virtue of section 30 of the Countryside Act 1968 (riding of pedal cycles on bridleways),

1968 c. 41.

(b) it subsists over the whole or part of a way any part of which is in an area which, immediately before 1st April 1965, formed part of the administrative county of London,

(c) it is a public right of way of such other description as may be specified in regulations made (as respects England) by the Secretary of State or (as respects Wales) by the National Assembly for Wales, or

(d) it subsists over land so specified.

(6) Regulations under subsection (1)(d) or (e) or (5)(c) or (d) shall be made by statutory instrument, and a statutory instrument containing such regulations made by the Secretary of State shall be subject to annulment in pursuance of a resolution of either House of Parliament.

55.—(1) Subject to subsections (2) and (3), the public shall, as from the day after the cut-off date, have a right of way on horseback or leading a horse over any way which—

   (a) was immediately before 1st January 1949 either a footpath or a bridleway, and

   (b) is, throughout the period beginning with the commencement of this section and ending with the cut-off date,

a footpath which is shown in a definitive map and statement as a bridleway.

(2) Subsection (1) has effect subject to the operation of any enactment or instrument (whether coming into operation before or after the cut-off date), and to the effect of any event otherwise within section 53(3)(a) of the 1981 Act, whereby a highway is authorised to be stopped up, diverted, widened or extended; and subsection (1) applies accordingly to any way as so diverted, widened or extended.

(3) Subsection (1) does not apply in relation to any way which is, or is part of, a footpath any part of which is in an area which, immediately before 1st April 1965, formed part of the administrative county of London.

(4) Any right of way over a way by virtue of subsection (1) is subject to any condition or limitation to which the public right of way on foot over that way was subject on the cut-off date.

(5) Where—

   (a) by virtue of regulations under section 56(2) an order under Part III of the 1981 Act takes effect after the cut-off date in relation to any footpath which, at the cut-off date was shown in a definitive map and statement as a bridleway,

   (b) the regulations do not prevent subsection (1) from having effect after the cut-off date in relation to that footpath, and

   (c) if the order had taken effect before that date, that footpath would not have fallen within subsection (1),

all rights over that way which exist only by virtue of subsection (1) shall be extinguished when the order takes effect.

(6) In this section "cut-off date" has the meaning given in section 56.

56.—(1) The cut-off date for the purposes of sections 53 and 55 is, subject to regulations under subsection (2), 1st January 2026.

(2) The Secretary of State (as respects England) or the National Assembly for Wales (as respects Wales) may make regulations—

   (a) substituting as the cut-off date for the purposes of those sections a date later than the date specified in subsection (1) or for the time being substituted under this paragraph;

   (b) containing such transitional provisions or savings as appear to the Secretary of State or the National Assembly for Wales (as the case may be) to be necessary or expedient in connection with the operation of those sections, including in particular their operation in relation to any way as respects which—

      (i) on the cut-off date an application for an order under section 53(2) of the 1981 Act is pending,

(ii) on that date an order under Part III of that Act has been made but not confirmed, or

(iii) after that date such an order or any provision of such an order is to any extent quashed.

(3) Regulations under subsection (2)(a)—

(a) may specify different dates for different areas; but

(b) may not specify a date later than 1st January 2031, except as respects an area within subsection (4).

(4) An area is within this subsection if it is in—

(a) the Isles of Scilly, or

1949 c. 97.

(b) an area which, at any time before the repeal by section 73 of the 1981 Act of sections 27 to 34 of the National Parks and Access to the Countryside Act 1949—

(i) was excluded from the operation of those sections by virtue of any provision of the 1949 Act, or

(ii) would have been so excluded but for a resolution having effect under section 35(2) of that Act.

(5) Where by virtue of regulations under subsection (2) there are different cut-off dates for areas into which different parts of any highway extend, the cut-off date in relation to that highway is the later or latest of those dates.

(6) Regulations under this section shall be made by statutory instrument, and a statutory instrument containing such regulations made by the Secretary of State shall be subject to annulment in pursuance of a resolution of either House of Parliament.

Creation, stopping up and diversion of highways

Creation, stopping up and diversion of highways.

1980 c. 66.

57. The Highways Act 1980 (in this Act referred to as "the 1980 Act") has effect subject to the amendments in Part I of Schedule 6 (which relate to the creation, stopping up and diversion of highways); and Part II of that Schedule (which contains consequential amendments of other Acts) has effect.

Application for path creation order for purposes of Part I.

58.—(1) An application for the making of a public path creation order under section 26(2) of the 1980 Act for the purpose of enabling the public to obtain access to any access land (within the meaning of Part I) or of facilitating such access, may be made—

(a) by the Countryside Agency to the Secretary of State, or

(b) by the Countryside Council for Wales to the National Assembly for Wales.

(2) Before making a request under subsection (1), the body making the request shall have regard to any rights of way improvement plan prepared by any local highway authority whose area includes land over which the proposed footpath or bridleway would be created.

Effect of Part I on powers to stop up or divert highways.

59.—(1) This section applies to any power to stop up or divert a highway of any description or to make or confirm an order authorising the stopping up or diversion of a highway of any description; and in the following provisions of this section—

(a) "the relevant authority" means the person exercising the power, and

(b) "the existing highway" means the highway to be stopped up or diverted.

(2) Where the relevant authority is required (expressly or by implication) to consider—

(a) whether the existing highway is unnecessary, or is needed for public use,

(b) whether an alternative highway should be provided, or

(c) whether any public right of way should be reserved,

the relevant authority, in considering that question, is not to regard the fact that any land is access land in respect of which the right conferred by section 2(1) is exercisable as reducing the need for the existing highway, for the provision of an alternative highway or for the reservation of a public right of way.

(3) Where—

(a) the existing highway is situated on, or in the vicinity of, any access land, and

(b) the relevant authority is required (expressly or by implication) to consider the extent (if any) to which the existing highway would, apart from the exercise of the power, be likely to be used by the public,

the relevant authority, in considering that question, is to have regard, in particular, to the extent to which the highway would be likely to be used by the public at any time when the right conferred by section 2(1) is not exercisable in relation to the access land.

(4) In this section "access land" has the same meaning as in Part I.

Rights of way improvement plans

60.—(1) Every local highway authority other than an inner London authority shall, within five years after the commencement of this section, prepare and publish a plan, to be known as a rights of way improvement plan, containing— *Rights of way improvement plans.*

(a) the authority's assessment of the matters specified in subsection (2),

(b) a statement of the action they propose to take for the management of local rights of way, and for securing an improved network of local rights of way, with particular regard to the matters dealt with in the assessment, and

(c) such other material as the Secretary of State (as respects England) or the National Assembly for Wales (as respects Wales) may direct.

(2) The matters referred to in subsection (1)(a) are—

(a) the extent to which local rights of way meet the present and likely future needs of the public,

(b) the opportunities provided by local rights of way (and in particular by those within paragraph (a) of the definition in subsection (5)) for exercise and other forms of open-air recreation and the enjoyment of the authority's area,

(c) the accessibility of local rights of way to blind or partially sighted persons and others with mobility problems, and

(d) such other matters relating to local rights of way as the Secretary of State (as respects England) or the National Assembly for Wales (as respects Wales) may direct.

(3) An authority by whom a rights of way improvement plan is published shall, not more than ten years after first publishing it and subsequently at intervals of not more than ten years—

(a) make a new assessment of the matters specified in subsection (2), and

(b) review the plan and decide whether to amend it.

(4) On such a review the authority shall—

(a) if they decide to amend the plan, publish it as amended, and

(b) if they decide to make no amendments to it, publish a report of their decision and of their reasons for it.

(5) In this section—

"cycle track"—

(a) means a way over which the public have the following, but no other, rights of way, that is to say, a right of way on pedal cycles (other than pedal cycles which are motor vehicles within the meaning of the Road Traffic Act 1988) with or without a right of way on foot; but

(b) does not include a way in or by the side of a highway consisting of or comprising a made-up carriageway (within the meaning of the 1980 Act);

"inner London authority" means Transport for London, the council of an inner London borough or the Common Council of the City of London;

"local highway authority" has the same meaning as in the 1980 Act;

"local rights of way" in relation to a local highway authority, means—

(a) the footpaths, cycle tracks, bridleways and restricted byways within the authority's area, and

(b) the ways within the authority's area which are shown in a definitive map and statement as restricted byways or byways open to all traffic.

(6) In subsection (5) the definition of "local rights of way" has effect until the commencement of section 47 with the substitution for the references to restricted byways and to ways shown in a definitive map and statement as restricted byways of a reference to ways shown in a definitive map and statement as roads used as public paths.

1988 c. 52.

Rights of way improvement plans: supplemental.

61.—(1) Before preparing or reviewing a rights of way improvement plan, and in particular in making any assessment under section 60(1)(a) or (3)(a), a local highway authority shall consult—

(a) each local highway authority whose area adjoins their area;

(b) each district council, and each parish or community council, whose area is within their area;

(c) the National Park authority for a National Park any part of which is within their area;

(d) where any part of the Broads is within their area, the Broads Authority;

(e) any local access forum established for their area or any part of it;

(f) the Countryside Agency or the Countryside Council for Wales (as appropriate);

(g) such persons as the Secretary of State (as respects England) or the National Assembly for Wales (as respects Wales) may by regulations prescribe in relation to the local highway authority's area; and

(h) such other persons as the local highway authority may consider appropriate.

(2) In preparing or amending a rights of way improvement plan, a local highway authority shall—

(a) publish a draft of the plan or of the plan as amended,

(b) publish, in two or more local newspapers circulating in their area, notice of how a copy of the draft can be inspected or obtained and how representations on it can be made to them, and

(c) consider any representations made in accordance with the notice.

(3) As regards their rights of way improvement plan, any draft plan on which representations may be made and any report under section 60(4)(b), a local highway authority shall—

(a) keep a copy available for inspection free of charge at all reasonable times at their principal offices, and

(b) supply a copy to any person who requests one, either free of charge or on payment of a reasonable charge determined by the authority.

(4) Local highway authorities shall, in carrying out their functions under section 60 and this section, have regard to such guidance as may from time to time be given to them by the Secretary of State (as respects England) or the National Assembly for Wales (as respects Wales).

(5) A local highway authority may make arrangements with—

(a) any district council whose area is within their area, or

(b) the National Park authority for a National Park any part of which is within their area,

for the functions of the local highway authority under section 60 and this section so far as relating to the area of that council or to the part of the Park within the local highway authority's area, to be discharged jointly by the local highway authority and by that council or National Park authority.

(6) Regulations under subsection (1)(g) shall be made by statutory instrument, and a statutory instrument containing such regulations made by the Secretary of State shall be subject to annulment in pursuance of a resolution of either House of Parliament.

(7) In this section—

"local highway authority" has the same meaning as in the 1980 Act;

PART II
1988 c. 4.

"the Broads" has the same meaning as in the Norfolk and Suffolk Broads Act 1988.

Application of ss. 60 and 61 to inner London.

62.—(1) The council of an inner London borough or the Common Council of the City of London may by resolution adopt sections 60 and 61 as respects their area or any part of it which is specified in the resolution.

(2) On the passing by any authority of a resolution under subsection (1), sections 60 and 61 shall, as respects their area or the part of it specified in the resolution, apply in relation to that authority—

(a) as they apply in relation to a local highway authority other than an inner London authority, but

(b) with the substitution for the reference in subsection (1) of section 60 to the commencement of that section of a reference to the date on which the resolution comes into operation.

Removal of obstructions from highways

Enforcement of duty to prevent obstructions.

63.—(1) After section 130 of the 1980 Act there is inserted—

"Notices to enforce duty regarding public paths.

130A.—(1) Any person who alleges, as respects any highway for which a local highway authority other than an inner London authority are the highway authority—

(a) that the highway falls within subsection (2) below, and

(b) that it is obstructed by an obstruction to which this section applies,

may serve on the highway authority notice requesting them to secure the removal of the obstruction from the highway.

(2) A highway is within this subsection if it is—

(a) a footpath, bridleway, or restricted byway, or

(b) a way shown in a definitive map and statement as a restricted byway or a byway open to all traffic.

(3) Subject to subsection (4) below, this section applies to an obstruction of the highway if the obstruction is without lawful authority and either—

(a) the powers conferred by section 143, 149 or 154 below are exercisable in respect of it, or

(b) it is of a description prescribed by regulations made by the Secretary of State and the authority have power (otherwise than under any of those sections) to secure its removal.

(4) This section does not apply to an obstruction if—

(a) it is or forms part of—

(i) a building (whether temporary or permanent) or works for the construction of a building, or

(ii) any other structure (including a tent, caravan, vehicle or other temporary or movable structure) which is designed, adapted or used for human habitation,

(b) an order may be made in respect of it under section 56 above, or

(c) the presence of any person constitutes the obstruction.

(5) A person serving a notice under subsection (1) above must include in the notice the name and address, if known to him, of any person who it appears to him may be for the time being responsible for the obstruction.

(6) A highway authority on whom a notice under subsection (1) above is served shall, within one month from the date of service of the notice, serve—

(a) on every person whose name and address is, pursuant to subsection (5) above, included in the notice and, so far as reasonably practicable, on every other person who it appears to them may be for the time being responsible for the obstruction, a notice informing that person that a notice under subsection (1) above has been served in relation to the obstruction and stating what, if any, action the authority propose to take, and

(b) on the person who served the notice under subsection (1) above, a notice containing the name and address of each person on whom notice is served under paragraph (a) above and stating what, if any, action the authority propose to take in relation to the obstruction.

(7) For the purposes of this section the persons for the time being responsible for an obstruction include the owner and any other person who for the time being—

(a) has possession or control of it, or

(b) may be required to remove it.

(8) A notice under subsection (1) or (6) above shall be in such form and contain such information as may be prescribed by regulations made by the Secretary of State.

(9) In this section "inner London authority" means Transport for London, the council of an inner London borough or the Common Council of the City of London.

(10) Subsection (2) above has effect until the commencement of section 47 of the Countryside and Rights of Way Act 2000 with the substitution for the references to a restricted byway and to a way shown in a definitive map and statement as a restricted byway of a reference to a way shown in a definitive map and statement as a road used as a public path.

Orders following notice under section 130A.

130B.—(1) Where a notice under section 130A(1) above has been served on a highway authority in relation to any obstruction, the person who served it, if not satisfied that the obstruction has been removed, may apply to a magistrates' court in accordance with section 130C below for an order under this section.

(2) An order under this section is an order requiring the highway authority to take, within such reasonable period as may be fixed by the order, such steps as may be specified in the order for securing the removal of the obstruction.

(3) An order under this section shall not take effect—

(a) until the end of the period of twenty-one days from the day on which the order is made; or

(b) if an appeal is brought in respect of the order within that period (whether by way of appeal to the Crown Court or by way of case stated for the opinion of the High Court), until the final determination or withdrawal of the appeal.

(4) Subject to subsection (5) below, the court may make an order under this section if it is satisfied—

(a) that the obstruction is one to which section 130A above applies or, in a case falling within subsection (4)(a)(ii) of that section, is one to which that section would apply but for the obstruction having become used for human habitation since service of the notice relating to it under subsection (1) of that section,

(b) that the way obstructed is a highway within subsection (2) of that section, and

(c) that the obstruction significantly interferes with the exercise of public rights of way over that way.

(5) No order shall be made under this section if the highway authority satisfy the court—

(a) that the fact that the way obstructed is a highway within section 130A(2) above is seriously disputed,

(b) on any other grounds, that they have no duty under section 130(3) above to secure the removal of the obstruction, or

(c) that, under arrangements which have been made by the authority, its removal will be secured within a reasonable time, having regard to the number and seriousness of obstructions in respect of which they have such a duty.

(6) A highway authority against whom an order is made under this section shall, as soon as practicable after the making of the order, cause notice of the order and of the right to appeal against it to be displayed in such manner and at such places on the highway concerned as may be prescribed by regulations made by the Secretary of State, and the notice shall be in such form and contain such information as may be so prescribed.

(7) An order under this section may be varied on the application of the highway authority to whom it relates.

Section 130B:
procedure.

130C.—(1) A person proposing to make an application under section 130B above shall before making the application serve notice of his intention to do so on the highway authority concerned.

(2) A notice under subsection (1) above shall be in such form and contain such information as may be prescribed by regulations made by the Secretary of State.

(3) The notice may not be served before the end of two months beginning with the date of service on the highway authority of the notice under section 130A(1) above ("the request notice").

(4) An application in respect of which notice has been served under subsection (1) above may be made at any time—

    (a) after the end of five days beginning with the date of service of that notice, and

    (b) before the end of six months beginning with the date of service on the highway authority of the request notice.

(5) On making the application the applicant must give notice to the court of the names and addresses of which notice was given to the applicant under section 130A(6)(b) above.

(6) On the hearing of the application any person who is, within the meaning of section 130A above, a person for the time being responsible for the obstruction to which the application relates has a right to be heard as respects the matters mentioned in section 130B(4) above.

(7) Notice of the hearing, of the right to be heard under subsection (6) above and of the right to appeal against a decision on the application shall be given by the court to each person whose name and address is notified to the court under subsection (5) above.

Section 130B:
costs.

130D. Where an application under section 130B above is dismissed by virtue of paragraph (a), (b) or (c) of subsection (5) of that section, the court, in determining whether and if so how to exercise its power under section 64(1) of the Magistrates' Courts Act 1980 (costs), shall have particular regard to any failure by the highway authority to give the applicant appropriate notice of, and information about, the grounds relied on by the authority under that paragraph."

1980 c. 43.

(2) In section 317 of the 1980 Act (appeals to the Crown Court from decisions of magistrates' courts) after subsection (2) there is inserted—

"(3) Any person who, in relation to the decision of a magistrates' court on an application under section 130B above, does not fall within subsection (1) above but—

    (a) is, within the meaning of section 130A above, a person for the time being responsible for the obstruction to which the application related, or

(b) when the application was heard, was such a person and was, or claimed to be, heard on the application,

may appeal to the Crown Court against the decision on any ground relating to the matters mentioned in section 130B(4) above."

Power to order offender to remove obstruction.

64.—(1) After section 137 of the 1980 Act (penalty for wilful obstruction) there is inserted—

"Power to order offender to remove obstruction.

137ZA.—(1) Where a person is convicted of an offence under section 137 above in respect of the obstruction of a highway and it appears to the court that—

(a) the obstruction is continuing, and

(b) it is in that person's power to remove the cause of the obstruction,

the court may, in addition to or instead of imposing any punishment, order him to take, within such reasonable period as may be fixed by the order, such steps as may be specified in the order for removing the cause of the obstruction.

(2) The time fixed by an order under subsection (1) above may be extended or further extended by order of the court on an application made before the end of the time as originally fixed or as extended under this subsection, as the case may be.

(3) If a person fails without reasonable excuse to comply with an order under subsection (1) above, he is guilty of an offence and liable to a fine not exceeding level 5 on the standard scale; and if the offence is continued after conviction he is guilty of a further offence and liable to a fine not exceeding one-twentieth of that level for each day on which the offence is so continued.

(4) Where, after a person is convicted of an offence under subsection (3) above, the highway authority for the highway concerned exercise any power to remove the cause of the obstruction, they may recover from that person the amount of any expenses reasonably incurred by them in, or in connection with, doing so.

(5) A person against whom an order is made under subsection (1) above is not liable under section 137 above in respect of the obstruction concerned—

(a) during the period fixed under that subsection or any extension under subsection (2) above, or

(b) during any period fixed under section 311(1) below by a court before whom he is convicted of an offence under subsection (3) above in respect of the order."

(2) Subsection (1) does not have effect in relation to any offence under section 137 of the 1980 Act committed before the commencement of this section.

65. In section 154 of the 1980 Act (cutting or felling etc. trees etc. that overhang or are a danger to roads or footpaths) in subsection (1) after "public lamp," there is inserted "or overhangs a highway so as to endanger or obstruct the passage of horse-riders,".

Overhanging vegetation obstructing horse-riders.

Miscellaneous

66.—(1) In section 22 of the Road Traffic Regulation Act 1984 (traffic regulation for special areas in the countryside), in subsection (1)(a)—

(a) the words "(other than Greater London)" are omitted,

(b) at the end of paragraph (vi), the word "or" is omitted, and

(c) before the word "and" at the end of paragraph (vii) there is inserted—

"or

(viii) a site of special scientific interest (within the meaning of the Wildlife and Countryside Act 1981);".

Making of traffic regulation orders for purposes of conserving natural beauty, etc.
1984 c. 27.

(2) In subsection (2) of that section, for "the paragraphs of subsection (1) of that section" there is substituted "paragraphs (a) to (g) of subsection (1) of that section and referred to in section 6(1)(b) of this Act".

(3) After subsection (4) of that section there is inserted—

"(5) In subsection (2) above the reference to conserving the natural beauty of an area shall be construed as including a reference to conserving its flora, fauna and geological and physiographical features.".

(4) After that section there is inserted—

"Traffic regulation on certain roads for purpose of conserving natural beauty.

22A.—(1) This section applies to roads other than—

(a) roads to which section 22 of this Act applies,

(b) special roads, or

(c) any road which is a trunk road, a classified road, a GLA road, a cycle track, a bridleway or a footpath, as those expressions are defined by section 329 of the Highways Act 1980.

1980 c. 66.

(2) This Act shall have effect as respects roads to which this section applies as if, in relation to the making of provision with respect to vehicular traffic, the list of purposes for which a traffic regulation order under section 1 of this Act may be made, as set out in paragraphs (a) to (g) of subsection (1) of that section and referred to in section 6(1)(b) of this Act, included the purpose of conserving or enhancing the natural beauty of the area.

(3) In subsection (2) above the reference to conserving the natural beauty of an area shall be construed as including a reference to conserving its flora, fauna and geological and physiographical features."

67. Schedule 7 (which makes amendments relating to the driving of mechanically propelled vehicles elsewhere than on roads) has effect.

Prohibition on driving mechanically propelled vehicles elsewhere than on roads.

68.—(1) This section applies to a way which the owner or occupier (from time to time) of any premises has used as a means of access for vehicles to the premises, if that use of the way—

> (a) was an offence under an enactment applying to the land crossed by the way, but

> (b) would otherwise have been sufficient to create on or after the prescribed date, and to keep in existence, an easement giving a right of way for vehicles.

(2) Regulations may provide, as respects a way to which this section applies, for the creation in accordance with the regulations, on the application of the owner of the premises concerned and on compliance by him with prescribed requirements, of an easement subsisting at law for the benefit of the premises and giving a right of way for vehicles over that way.

(3) An easement created in accordance with the regulations is subject to any enactment or rule of law which would apply to such an easement granted by the owner of the land.

(4) The regulations may in particular—

> (a) require that, where an application is made after the relevant use of the way has ceased, it is to be made within a specified time,

> (b) specify grounds on which objections may be made and the procedure to apply to the making of objections,

> (c) require any matter to be referred to and determined by the Lands Tribunal, and make provision as to procedure and costs,

> (d) make provision as to the payment of any amount by the owner of the premises concerned to any person or into court and as to the time when any payment is to be made,

> (e) provide for the determination of any such amount,

> (f) make provision as to the date on which any easement is created,

> (g) specify any limitation to which the easement is subject,

> (h) provide for the easement to include any specified right incidental to the right of way,

> (i) make different provision for different circumstances.

(5) In this section—

> "enactment" includes an enactment in a local or private Act and a byelaw, regulation or other provision having effect under an enactment;

> "owner", in relation to any premises, means—

>> (a) a person, other than a mortgagee not in possession, who is for the time being entitled to dispose of the fee simple of the premises, whether in possession or in reversion, or

>> (b) a tenant under a long lease, within the meaning of the Landlord and Tenant Act 1987;

> "prescribed" means prescribed by regulations;

> "regulations" means regulations made, as respects England, by the Secretary of State and, as respects Wales, by the National Assembly for Wales.

1987 c. 31.

(6) Regulations under this section shall be made by statutory instrument, and no such regulations shall be made by the Secretary of State unless a draft has been laid before, and approved by a resolution of, each House of Parliament.

69.—(1) In section 147 of the 1980 Act (power to authorise erection of stiles etc on footpath or bridleway) after subsection (2) there is inserted—

Erection or improvement of stiles, etc.

"(2A) In exercising their powers under subsection (2) above a competent authority shall have regard to the needs of persons with mobility problems.

(2B) The Secretary of State may issue guidance to competent authorities as to matters to be taken into account for the purposes of subsection (2) above; and in exercising their powers under subsection (2) above competent authorities shall have regard to any such guidance issued to them."

(2) In subsection (5) of that section, at the end there is inserted "or for the breeding or keeping of horses."

(3) After that section there is inserted—

"Agreements relating to improvements for benefit of persons with mobility problems.

147ZA.—(1) With respect to any relevant structure, a competent authority may enter into an agreement with the owner, lessee or occupier of the land on which the structure is situated which provides—

(a) for the carrying out by the owner, lessee or occupier of any qualifying works and the payment by the competent authority of the whole or any part of the costs incurred by him in carrying out those works, or

(b) for the carrying out by the competent authority of any qualifying works at their own expense or subject to the payment by the owner, lessee or occupier of the whole or any part of the costs incurred in carrying out those works.

(2) In this section—

(a) "competent authority" has the same meaning as in section 147 above,

(b) "relevant structure" means a stile, gate or other structure which—

(i) is authorised by a condition or limitation subject to which the public right of way over the footpath or bridleway was created, or

(ii) is authorised under section 147 above,

but does not include a structure to which an agreement falling within section 146(5)(b) above relates, and

(c) "qualifying works", in relation to a relevant structure, means works for replacing or improving the structure which will result in a structure that is safer or more convenient for persons with mobility problems.

(3) An agreement under this section may include such conditions as the competent authority think fit.

(4) Those conditions may in particular include conditions expressed to have enduring effect—

(a) for the maintenance of the structure as replaced or improved, and

(b) for enabling the public right of way to be exercised without undue inconvenience to the public.

(5) Where an agreement under this section has been entered into in relation to any structure—

(a) the public right of way is to be deemed to be subject to a condition that the structure as replaced or improved may be erected and maintained in accordance with the agreement so long as any conditions included by virtue of subsection (4) above are complied with,

(b) in a case falling within subsection (2)(b)(i) above, as from the effective date the previous condition or limitation relating to the relevant structure shall cease to have effect, and

(c) in a case falling within subsection (2)(b)(ii) above, as from the effective date the previous authorisation under section 147 above shall cease to have effect in relation to the relevant structure.

(6) In subsection (5) above "the effective date" means—

(a) the first anniversary of the day on which the agreement was entered into, or

(b) such earlier date as may be specified for the purposes of this subsection in the agreement.

(7) For the purposes of section 143 above, any stile, gate or other structure replaced or improved in pursuance of an agreement under this section is to be deemed to be erected under this section only if any conditions included by virtue of subsection (4) above are complied with.

(8) A competent authority may not enter into an agreement under this section except with the consent of every owner, lessee or occupier of the land on which the relevant structure is situated who is not a party to the agreement.

(9) The Secretary of State may issue guidance to competent authorities as to matters to be taken into account for the purposes of this section; and in exercising their powers under this section competent authorities shall have regard to any such guidance issued to them."

(4) In section 146 of the 1980 Act (duty to maintain stiles etc. on footpaths and bridleways) in subsection (5), before the word "or" at the end of paragraph (a) there is inserted—

"(aa) if any conditions for the maintenance of the structure imposed by virtue of subsection (4) of section 147ZA below are for the time being in force under that section,".

(5) In section 344 of the 1980 Act (application to Isles of Scilly) in subsection (2)(a) after "147," there is inserted "147ZA,".

70.—(1) In section 66(3) of the 1980 Act (works for safeguarding persons using footpaths)—

> (a) after "footpath" there is inserted "or bridleway", and
>
> (b) after "barriers," there is inserted "posts,".

Minor amendments.

(2) In section 134 of that Act, subsection (5) (which limits the persons who may bring proceedings for failure to restore a public path disturbed by ploughing etc.) is omitted.

(3) In section 300 of that Act (right of local authorities to use vehicles and appliances on footways and bridleways), in subsection (1) after "verges," there is inserted "for preventing or removing obstructions to them or otherwise preventing or abating nuisances or other interferences with them,".

(4) In section 21(2)(b) of the Road Traffic Act 1988 (defence to charge of driving or parking on cycle track for highway authority vehicles), after "verges" there is inserted ", or the preventing or removing of obstructions to the cycle track or the preventing or abating in any other way of nuisances or other interferences with the cycle track,".

1988 c. 52.

71.—(1) The Secretary of State (as respects England) or the National Assembly for Wales (as respects Wales) may make regulations requiring local highway authorities of a description specified in the regulations to publish reports on the performance of any of their functions so far as relating to local rights of way (whether or not those functions are conferred on them as highway authorities).

Reports on functions relating to rights of way.

(2) Subsection (1) is without prejudice to section 230 of the Local Government Act 1972 (reports and returns).

1972 c. 70.

(3) Regulations under subsection (1) may prescribe the information to be given in such reports and how and when reports are to be published.

(4) Regulations under subsection (1) shall be made by statutory instrument, and a statutory instrument containing such regulations made by the Secretary of State shall be subject to annulment in pursuance of a resolution of either House of Parliament.

(5) In this section—

> "local highway authority" has the same meaning as in the 1980 Act, except that it does not include Transport for London; and
>
> "local rights of way" has the same meaning as in section 60.

72.—(1) In this Part, unless a contrary intention appears—

> (a) "restricted byway" and "restricted byway rights" have the meaning given by section 48(4);
>
> (b) expressions which are defined for the purposes of Part III of the 1981 Act by section 66(1) of that Act have the same meaning as in that Part.

Interpretation of Part II.

(2) In this Part any reference to a highway includes a reference to part of a highway.

PART III

NATURE CONSERVATION AND WILDLIFE PROTECTION

The Nature Conservancy Council for England

The Nature Conservancy Council for England: change of name.

73.—(1) The Nature Conservancy Council for England shall be known instead as English Nature.

(2) For any reference to the Nature Conservancy Council for England—

(a) in any provision of a local Act or subordinate legislation, or

(b) in any other instrument or document,

there is substituted, as respects any time after the commencement of subsection (1), a reference to English Nature.

(3) Any reference to English Nature in this Act (apart from this section), or in any instrument under this Act, shall be construed, in relation to any time before the commencement of subsection (1), as a reference to the Nature Conservancy Council for England.

(4) Schedule 8 (which makes amendments consequential on subsection (1)) has effect.

Biological diversity

Conservation of biological diversity.
1975 c. 26.

74.—(1) It is the duty of—

(a) any Minister of the Crown (within the meaning of the Ministers of the Crown Act 1975),

(b) any Government department, and

(c) the National Assembly for Wales,

in carrying out his or its functions, to have regard, so far as is consistent with the proper exercise of those functions, to the purpose of conserving biological diversity in accordance with the Convention.

(2) The Secretary of State, as respects England, and the National Assembly for Wales, as respects Wales, shall each publish a list of, or lists which together comprise, the living organisms and types of habitat which in the opinion of the Secretary of State or the Assembly (as the case may be) are of principal importance for the purpose mentioned in subsection (1).

(3) Without prejudice to subsection (1), it is the duty of a listing authority to take, or to promote the taking by others of, such steps as appear to the authority to be reasonably practicable to further the conservation of the living organisms and types of habitat included in any list published by the authority under this section.

(4) Before publishing the list or lists required by subsection (2) the listing authority shall consult the appropriate conservation body as to the living organisms or types of habitat to be included in the list or lists.

(5) Each listing authority shall, in consultation with the appropriate conservation body—

    (a) keep under review any list published by the authority under this section,

    (b) make such revisions of any such list as appear to the authority to be appropriate, and

    (c) publish any list so revised.

(6) A duty under this section to publish a list is a duty to publish it in such manner as the listing authority thinks fit.

(7) In this section—

"appropriate conservation body" means—

    (a) as respects England, English Nature,

    (b) as respects Wales, the Countryside Council for Wales;

"biological diversity" has the same meaning as in the Convention;

"conservation" in relation to a living organism or type of habitat, includes the restoration or enhancement of a population or habitat;

"the Convention" means the United Nations Environmental Programme Convention on Biological Diversity of 1992;

"habitat" has the same meaning as in the Convention;

"listing authority"—

    (a) in relation to a list which the Secretary of State is required to publish under this section, means the Secretary of State;

    (b) in relation to a list which the National Assembly for Wales is required to publish under this section, means the National Assembly for Wales.

Sites of special scientific interest

75.—(1) Schedule 9 (which makes amendments of the 1981 Act to change the law relating to sites of special scientific interest, including provision as to offences) has effect.

Sites of special scientific interest.

(2) A notification under section 23 of the National Parks and Access to the Countryside Act 1949 (notification to local planning authorities of areas of special scientific interest) which by virtue of section 28(13) of the 1981 Act as originally enacted had effect as if given under section 28(1)(a) of that Act, shall cease to have effect.

1949 c. 97.

(3) In section 15(2) of the Countryside Act 1968 (which provides for agreements between the Nature Conservancy Council and those with interests in land which is included in an area of special scientific interest, or is adjacent to such land), for "adjacent" there is substituted "other".

1968 c. 41.

(4) After section 15 of the Countryside Act 1968 there is inserted—

"Compulsory purchase.

    15A.—(1) The Nature Conservancy Council may in circumstances set out in subsection (2) acquire compulsorily all or any part of the land referred to in section 15(2).

(2) The circumstances are—

(a) that the Nature Conservancy Council are satisfied that they are unable to conclude, on reasonable terms, such an agreement as is referred to in section 15(2), or

(b) that they have entered into such an agreement, but they are satisfied it has been breached in such a way that the flora, fauna or geological or physiographical features referred to there are not being conserved satisfactorily.

(3) A dispute about whether or not there has been a breach of the agreement for the purposes of subsection (2)(b) shall be determined by an arbitrator appointed by the Lord Chancellor.

(4) Where the Nature Conservancy Council have acquired land compulsorily under this section, they may—

(a) themselves take steps to conserve the flora, fauna or geological or physiographical features in question, or

(b) dispose of the land on terms designed to secure that those flora, fauna or features are satisfactorily conserved.

(5) In this section, "Nature Conservancy Council" means English Nature as respects land in England, and the Council as respects land in Wales."

Consequential amendments, transitional provisions and savings relating to s. 75.

76.—(1) Schedule 10 (which makes amendments of the 1981 Act consequential upon the substitution or repeal as respects England and Wales of certain sections in that Act, and also makes other consequential amendments) has effect.

(2) Schedule 11 (which makes transitional provisions and savings relating to the coming into force of section 75) has effect.

Ramsar sites

Ramsar sites.

77. After section 37 of the 1981 Act there is inserted—

"Ramsar sites.   37A.—(1) Where a wetland in Great Britain has been designated under paragraph 1 of article 2 of the Ramsar Convention for inclusion in the list of wetlands of international importance referred to in that article, the Secretary of State shall—

(a) notify English Nature if all or part of the wetland is in England;

(b) notify the Countryside Council for Wales if it is in Wales; or

(c) notify both of them if it is partly in England and partly in Wales.

(2) Subject to subsection (3), upon receipt of a notification under subsection (1), each body notified shall, in turn, notify—

(a) the local planning authority in whose area the wetland is situated;

(b) every owner and occupier of any of that wetland;

(c) the Environment Agency; and

(d) every relevant undertaker (within the meaning of section 4(1) of the Water Industry Act 1991) and every internal drainage board (within the meaning of section 61C(1) of the Land Drainage Act 1991) whose works, operations or activities may affect the wetland.

1991 c. 56.

1991 c. 59.

(3) English Nature and the Countryside Council for Wales may agree that in a case where the Secretary of State notifies both of them under subsection (1)(c), any notice under subsection (2) is to be sent by one or the other of them (and not both), so as to avoid duplicate notices under that subsection.

(4) Subject to subsection (5), the "Ramsar Convention" is the Convention on Wetlands of International Importance especially as Waterfowl Habitat signed at Ramsar on 2nd February 1971, as amended by—

(a) the Protocol known as the Paris Protocol done at Paris on 3rd December 1982; and

(b) the amendments known as the Regina Amendments adopted at the Extraordinary Conference of the Contracting Parties held at Regina, Saskatchewan, Canada, between 28th May and 3rd June 1987.

(5) If the Ramsar Convention is further amended after the passing of the Countryside and Rights of Way Act 2000, the reference to the Ramsar Convention in subsection (1) is to be taken after the entry into force of the further amendments as referring to that Convention as further amended (and the reference to paragraph 1 of article 2 is, if necessary, to be taken as referring to the appropriate successor provision)."

Limestone pavement orders

78.—(1) In section 34(4) of the 1981 Act (which provides for an offence in connection with land designated by a limestone pavement order), for "the statutory maximum" there is substituted "£20,000".

Limestone pavement orders: offence.

(2) Subsection (1) does not have effect in relation to any offence committed before the commencement of this section.

PART III

Payments under certain agreements

Payments under
agreements under
s.16 of 1949 Act
or s.15 of 1968
Act.
1949 c. 97.
1968 c. 41.

79. In section 50 of the 1981 Act (which makes provision relating to payments under section 16 of the National Parks and Access to the Countryside Act 1949 or section 15 of the Countryside Act 1968), in subsection (1)(a), for sub-paragraphs (i) and (ii) and the preceding word "to" there is substituted "to any person; or".

Powers of entry

Powers of entry.

80.—(1) Section 51 of the 1981 Act (powers of entry) is amended as follows.

(2) In subsection (1), for paragraphs (a) to (d) there is substituted—

"(a) to determine whether the land should be notified under section 28(1);

(b) to assess the condition of the flora, fauna, or geological or physiographical features by reason of which land which has been notified under section 28(1) is of special interest;

(c) to determine whether or not to offer to enter into an agreement under section 16 of the 1949 Act or section 15 of the 1968 Act in relation to the land;

(d) to ascertain whether a condition to which a consent referred to in section 28E(3)(a) was subject has been complied with in relation to the land;

(e) to ascertain whether an offence under section 28P or under byelaws made by virtue of section 28R is being, or has been, committed on or in relation to the land;

(f) to formulate a management scheme for the land or determine whether a management scheme (or a proposed management scheme) for the land should be modified;

(g) to prepare a management notice for the land;

(h) to ascertain whether the terms of an agreement under section 16 of the 1949 Act or section 15 of the 1968 Act in relation to the land, or the terms of a management scheme or the requirements of a management notice in relation to the land, have been complied with;

(i) to determine whether or not to offer to make a payment under section 28M in relation to the land;

(j) to determine any question in relation to the acquisition of the land by agreement or compulsorily;

(k) to determine any question in relation to compensation under section 20(3) of the 1949 Act as applied by section 28R of this Act;

(l) to ascertain whether an order should be made in relation to the land under section 34 or if an offence under that section is being, or has been, committed on the land;

(m) to ascertain whether an order should be made in relation to the land under section 42 or if an offence under that section is being, or has been, committed on the land;".

(3) After subsection (1) there is inserted—

"(1A) The power conferred by subsection (1) to enter land for any purpose includes power to enter for the same purpose any land other than that referred to in subsection (1).

(1B) More than one person may be authorised for the time being under subsection (1) to enter any land."

(4) In subsection (2)—

(a) in paragraph (a), for "paragraphs (a) and (b)" there is substituted "paragraphs (a) to (k)";

(b) in paragraph (b), for "paragraph (c)" there is substituted "paragraph (l)"; and

(c) in paragraph (c), for "paragraph (d)" there is substituted "paragraph (m)".

(5) For subsection (3)(b) there is substituted—

"(b) the purpose of the entry is to ascertain if an offence under section 28P, 34 or 42 is being, or has been, committed on or (as the case may be) in relation to that land."

(6) After subsection (3) there is inserted—

"(3A) A person acting in the exercise of a power conferred by subsection (1) may—

(a) use a vehicle or a boat to enter the land;

(b) take a constable with him if he reasonably believes he is likely to be obstructed;

(c) take with him equipment and materials needed for the purpose for which he is exercising the power of entry;

(d) take samples of the land and of anything on it.

(3B) If in the exercise of a power conferred by subsection (1) a person enters land which is unoccupied or from which the occupier is temporarily absent, he must on his departure leave it as effectively secured against unauthorised entry as he found it."

(7) After subsection (4) there is inserted—

"(5) It is the duty of a relevant authority to compensate any person who has sustained damage as a result of—

(a) the exercise of a power conferred by subsection (1) by a person authorised to do so by that relevant authority, or

(b) the failure of a person so authorised to perform the duty imposed on him by subsection (3B),

except where the damage is attributable to the fault of the person who sustained it; and any dispute as to a person's entitlement to compensation under this subsection or as to its amount shall be referred to an arbitrator to be appointed, in default of agreement, by the Secretary of State".

PART III

Enforcement of wildlife legislation

Enforcement of
wildlife legislation.

81.—(1) Schedule 12 to this Act (which contains amendments relating to offences and enforcement powers under Part I of the 1981 Act) has effect.

1972 c. 68.

(2) In relation to England and Wales, regulations under section 2(2) of the European Communities Act 1972 ("the 1972 Act") for the purpose of implementing any of the instruments mentioned in subsection (3) may, notwithstanding paragraph 1(1)(d) of Schedule 2 to the 1972 Act, create offences punishable on summary conviction with imprisonment for a term not exceeding six months.

(3) Those instruments are—

   (a) Council Directive 92/43/EEC on the conservation of natural habitats and of wild fauna and flora as amended by the Act of Accession to the European Union of Austria, Finland and Sweden and by Council Directive 97/62/EC;

   (b) Council Regulation 338/97/EC on the protection of species of wild fauna and flora by regulating the trade therein; and

   (c) Commission Regulation 939/97/EC on the implementation of the Council Regulation mentioned in paragraph (b).

PART IV

AREAS OF OUTSTANDING NATURAL BEAUTY

Designation of
areas.

82.—(1) Where it appears to the Countryside Agency (in this Part referred to as "the Agency") that an area which is in England but not in a National Park is of such outstanding natural beauty that it is desirable that the provisions of this Part relating to areas designated under this section should apply to it, the Agency may, for the purpose of conserving and enhancing the natural beauty of the area, by order designate the area for the purposes of this Part as an area of outstanding natural beauty.

(2) Where it appears to the Countryside Council for Wales (in this Part referred to as "the Council") that an area which is in Wales but not in a National Park is of such outstanding natural beauty that it is desirable that the provisions of this Part relating to areas designated under this section should apply to it, the Council may, for the purpose of conserving and enhancing the natural beauty of the area, by order designate the area for the purposes of this Part as an area of outstanding natural beauty.

(3) In this Part "area of outstanding natural beauty" means an area designated under this section as an area of outstanding natural beauty.

Procedure for
designation
orders.

83.—(1) Where the Agency or the Council propose to make an order under section 82, the Agency or the Council shall consult every local authority whose area includes any part of the area to which the proposed order is to relate.

(2) Before making the order, the Agency or the Council shall then publish, in the London Gazette and in one or more newspapers circulating in the area of every such local authority, notice that they propose to make the order, indicating the effect of the order and stating the time within which and manner in which representations with respect to the proposed order may be made to the Agency or the Council (as the case may be), and shall consider any representations duly made.

(3) An order under section 82 shall not come into operation unless and until confirmed—

    (a) in the case of an order made by the Agency, by the Secretary of State, or

    (b) in the case of an order made by the Council, by the National Assembly for Wales,

and, in submitting any such order to the Secretary of State or the Assembly, the Agency or Council shall forward to the Secretary of State or the Assembly any representations made by a local authority consulted under subsection (1) or made by any other person under subsection (2), other than representations to which effect is given by the order as submitted to the Secretary of State or the Assembly.

(4) The Secretary of State or the National Assembly for Wales may confirm an order submitted to him or it under this section either as submitted or with such modifications as the Secretary of State or the Assembly thinks expedient.

(5) Before refusing to confirm an order under section 82, or determining to confirm it with modifications, the Secretary of State shall consult the Agency and every local authority whose area includes any land to which the order as submitted, or as proposed to be modified, relates.

(6) Before refusing to confirm an order under section 82, or determining to confirm it with modifications, the National Assembly for Wales shall consult the Council and every local authority whose area includes any land to which the order as submitted, or as proposed to be modified, relates.

(7) An order under section 82 may be revoked or varied by a subsequent order under that section.

(8) Without prejudice to the powers of the Agency or the Council to vary an order under section 82, the Secretary of State (as respects England) or the National Assembly for Wales (as respects Wales) may by order vary any order under that section made by the Agency or the Council; and subsection (1) applies to any order under section 82 made by the Secretary of State or the Assembly by virtue of this subsection with the substitution for references to the Agency of references to the Secretary of State and for references to the Council of references to the Assembly.

(9) It is the duty of the Agency and the Council to secure that copies of any order under section 82 relating to England or, as the case may be, to Wales, are available for inspection by the public at all reasonable times—

    (a) at the office of the Agency or, as the case may be, the Council,

    (b) at the offices of each local authority whose area includes any part of the area to which the order relates, and

    (c) at such other place or places in or near that area as the Agency or, as the case may be, the Council may determine.

84.—(1) The following provisions of the National Parks and Access to the Countryside Act 1949 (in this Part referred to as "the 1949 Act")—

    (a) section 6(4)(e) (duty of Agency or Council to give advice in connection with development matters),

    (b) section 9 (consultation in connection with development plan),

Functions of certain bodies in relation to areas of outstanding natural beauty.

1949 c. 97.

(c) section 64(5) (consultation in connection with access agreements), and

(d) section 65(5) and (5A) (consultation in connection with access orders),

apply in relation to areas of outstanding natural beauty as they apply in relation to National Parks.

(2) In section 6(4)(e) of the 1949 Act as it applies by virtue of subsection (1), "appropriate planning authority" means a local planning authority whose area consists of or includes the whole or any part of an area of outstanding natural beauty and includes a local authority, not being a local planning authority, by whom any powers of a local planning authority as respects an area of outstanding natural beauty are exercisable, whether under the 1949 Act or otherwise.

(3) Section 4A of the 1949 Act (which confers on the Council functions under Part II of that Act corresponding to those exercisable as respects England by the Agency) applies to the provisions mentioned in subsection (1)(a) and (b) for the purposes of their application to areas of outstanding natural beauty as that section applies for the purposes of Part II of the 1949 Act.

(4) A local planning authority whose area consists of or includes the whole or any part of an area of outstanding natural beauty has power, subject to subsections (5) and (6), to take all such action as appears to them expedient for the accomplishment of the purpose of conserving and enhancing the natural beauty of the area of outstanding natural beauty or so much of it as is included in their area.

(5) Nothing in this Part is to be taken to limit the generality of subsection (4); but in so far as the provisions of this Part or of the 1949 Act confer specific powers falling within that subsection those powers are to be exercised in accordance with those provisions and subject to any limitations expressed or implied in them.

(6) Without prejudice to the powers conferred by this Part, subsection (4) has effect only for the purpose of removing any limitation imposed by law on the capacity of a local planning authority by virtue of its constitution, and does not authorise any act or omission on the part of such an authority which apart from that subsection would be actionable at the suit of any person on any ground other than such a limitation.

1990 c. 8.

(7) In this section "local planning authority" has the same meaning as in the Town and Country Planning Act 1990.

General duty of public bodies etc.

85.—(1) In exercising or performing any functions in relation to, or so as to affect, land in an area of outstanding natural beauty, a relevant authority shall have regard to the purpose of conserving and enhancing the natural beauty of the area of outstanding natural beauty.

(2) The following are relevant authorities for the purposes of this section—

(a) any Minister of the Crown,

(b) any public body,

(c) any statutory undertaker,

(d) any person holding public office.

(3) In subsection (2)—

"public body" includes

     (a) a county council, county borough council, district council, parish council or community council;

     (b) a joint planning board within the meaning of section 2 of the Town and Country Planning Act 1990;   1990 c. 8.

     (c) a joint committee appointed under section 102(1)(b) of the Local Government Act 1972;   1972 c. 70.

"public office" means—

     (a) an office under Her Majesty;

     (b) an office created or continued in existence by a public general Act; or

     (c) an office the remuneration in respect of which is paid out of money provided by Parliament.

86.—(1) The Secretary of State (as respects England) or the National Assembly for Wales (as respects Wales) may—

Establishment of conservation boards.

    (a) in the case of any existing area of outstanding natural beauty, or

    (b) in connection with the designation of any area as an area of outstanding natural beauty,

by order establish a board (in this Part referred to as "a conservation board") to carry out in relation to that area the functions conferred on such a board by or under this Part.

(2) Schedule 13 (which relates to the constitution of conservation boards) has effect.

(3) Where the Secretary of State or the National Assembly for Wales considers it expedient for either of the purposes mentioned in section 87(1), an order under subsection (1) may—

    (a) provide for the transfer to the conservation board to which the order relates of any of the functions of local authorities, so far as relating to the area of outstanding natural beauty in question, or

    (b) provide for any function of a local authority, so far as relating to the area of outstanding natural beauty in question, to be exercisable concurrently by the local authority and by the conservation board.

(4) Subsection (3) does not apply to functions of a local authority under Part II, III, VII or XIII of the Town and Country Planning Act 1990.

(5) An order under subsection (1) may make further provision as to the constitution and administration of the conservation board to which it relates, including provision with respect to—

    (a) the appointment of members,

    (b) the removal and disqualification of members,

    (c) the conduct of members,

    (d) proceedings of the board,

    (e) the appointment of staff,

    (f) consultation with other public bodies,

    (g) records and documents of the board,

(h) the provision of information by the board, and

(i) complaints of maladministration.

(6) Before making an order under subsection (1) in relation to an area of outstanding natural beauty in England, the Secretary of State shall consult—

(a) the Agency, and

(b) every local authority whose area consists of or includes the whole or part of the area of outstanding natural beauty,

and shall not make the order unless satisfied that the majority of those local authorities consent.

(7) Before making an order under subsection (1) in relation to an area of outstanding natural beauty in Wales, the National Assembly for Wales shall consult—

(a) the Council, and

(b) every local authority whose area consists of or includes the whole or part of the area of outstanding natural beauty,

and shall not make the order unless satisfied that the majority of those local authorities consent.

(8) An order under subsection (1) which amends or revokes a previous order under that subsection establishing a conservation board—

(a) may be made only after consultation with the conservation board to which it relates (as well as the consultation required by subsection (6) or (7)), and

(b) in the case of an order revoking a previous order, may provide for the winding up of the board.

(9) Subject to any order under subsection (10), where there is a variation of the area of an area of outstanding natural beauty for which there is or is to be a conservation board, the area of outstanding natural beauty for which that board is or is to be the conservation board shall be taken, as from the time when the variation takes effect, to be that area as varied.

(10) Where provision is made for the variation of the area of an area of outstanding natural beauty for which there is or is to be a conservation board, the Secretary of State (as respects England) or the National Assembly for Wales (as respects Wales) may by order make such transitional provision as he or it thinks fit with respect to—

(a) any functions which, in relation to any area that becomes part of the area of outstanding natural beauty, are by virtue of the variation to become functions of that conservation board; and

(b) any functions which, in relation to any area that ceases to be part of the area of outstanding natural beauty, are by virtue of the variation to become functions of a person other than that conservation board.

General purposes and powers.

87.—(1) It is the duty of a conservation board, in the exercise of their functions, to have regard to—

(a) the purpose of conserving and enhancing the natural beauty of the area of outstanding natural beauty, and

(b) the purpose of increasing the understanding and enjoyment by the public of the special qualities of the area of outstanding natural beauty,

but if it appears to the board that there is a conflict between those purposes, they are to attach greater weight to the purpose mentioned in paragraph (a).

(2) A conservation board, while having regard to the purposes mentioned in subsection (1), shall seek to foster the economic and social well-being of local communities within the area of outstanding natural beauty, but without incurring significant expenditure in doing so, and shall for that purpose co-operate with local authorities and public bodies whose functions include the promotion of economic or social development within the area of outstanding natural beauty.

(3) Sections 37 and 38 of the Countryside Act 1968 (general duties as to the protection of interests of the countryside and the avoidance of pollution) apply to conservation boards as they apply to local authorities.   1968 c. 41.

(4) The powers of a conservation board include power to do anything which, in the opinion of the board, is calculated to facilitate, or is conducive or incidental to—

(a) the accomplishment of the purposes mentioned in subsection (1), or

(b) the carrying out of any functions conferred on it by virtue of any other provision of this Part or by virtue of any enactment not contained in this Part.

(5) The powers conferred on a conservation board by subsection (4) do not include—

(a) power to do anything in contravention of any restriction imposed by virtue of this Part in relation to any express power of the board, or

(b) power to raise money (whether by borrowing or otherwise) in a manner which is not authorised apart from that subsection,

but the things that may be done in exercise of those powers are not to be treated as excluding anything by reason only that it involves the expenditure, borrowing or lending of money or the acquisition or disposal of any property or rights.

(6) Schedule 14 (which relates to the supplemental and incidental powers of conservation boards) has effect.

(7) An order under section 86(1) may—

(a) make further provision with respect to the supplemental and incidental powers of the conservation board to which it relates or the limits on those powers, including provision relating to the borrowing of money, and

(b) provide for any enactment which relates to or limits the supplemental or incidental powers or duties of local authorities or relates to the conduct of, or transactions by, local authorities to apply in relation to the conservation board with such modifications as may be specified in the order.

88.—(1) Any power of the Secretary of State or the National Assembly for Wales to make an order under section 86(1) or (10) is exercisable by statutory instrument.

(2) No order shall be made under section 86(1) by the Secretary of State unless a draft of the order has been laid before, and approved by a resolution of, each House of Parliament.

(3) A statutory instrument containing an order made under section 86(10) by the Secretary of State shall be subject to annulment in pursuance of a resolution of either House of Parliament.

(4) If a draft of an order made under section 86(1) by the Secretary of State would, apart from this section, be treated for the purposes of the Standing Orders of either House of Parliament as a hybrid instrument, it shall proceed in that House as if it were not such an instrument.

(5) The power of the Secretary of State or the National Assembly for Wales to make an order under section 86(1) or (10) includes power to make such incidental, supplemental, consequential and transitional provision as the person making the order thinks necessary or expedient.

(6) The power of the Secretary of State or the National Assembly for Wales by an order under section 86(1) or (10) to make incidental, supplemental, consequential or transitional provision includes power for any incidental, supplemental, consequential or, as the case may be, transitional purpose—

　(a) to apply with or without modifications,

　(b) to extend, exclude or modify, or

　(c) to repeal or revoke with or without savings,

any enactment or any instrument made under any enactment.

(7) The provision that may be made for incidental, supplemental, consequential or transitional purposes in the case of any order under section 86(1) or (10) which—

　(a) establishes a conservation board or provides for the winding up of such a board, or

　(b) otherwise has the effect of transferring functions from one person to another or of providing for functions to become exercisable concurrently by two or more persons or to cease to be so exercisable,

includes provision for the transfer of property, rights and liabilities from one person to another.

(8) The power of the Secretary of State or the National Assembly for Wales under section 86(1) or (10) to provide by order for the transfer of any property, rights or liabilities, or to make transitional provision in connection with any such transfer or with any order by which functions become or cease to be exercisable by any conservation board, includes, in particular, power to provide—

　(a) for the management and custody of any transferred property (whether real or personal);

　(b) for any liabilities transferred to include liabilities under any enactment;

(c) for legal proceedings commenced by or against any person to be continued by or against a person to whom property, rights or liabilities are transferred or, as the case may be, any board or other authority by whom any functions are to become exercisable;

(d) for the transfer of staff, compensation for loss of office, pensions and other staffing matters; and

(e) for treating any person to whom a transfer of property, rights or liabilities is made or, as the case may be, by whom any functions are to become exercisable as, for some or all purposes, the same person in law as the person from whom the transfer is made or the authority by whom the functions have previously been exercisable.

(9) The power of the Secretary of State or the National Assembly for Wales to make an order under section 86(1) or (10) includes power to make different provision for different cases, including different provision for different areas or localities and for different boards.

(10) In this section "enactment" includes an enactment contained in an Act passed after this Act.

89.—(1) Every conservation board shall, within two years after the date on which they are established, prepare and publish a plan which formulates their policy for the management of their area of outstanding natural beauty and for the carrying out of their functions in relation to it.

Management plans.

(2) Subject to subsection (3), the relevant local authority in respect of an area of outstanding natural beauty shall, before the end of the period of three years beginning with whichever is the later of—

(a) the commencement of this section, or

(b) the date on which the area is designated as an area of outstanding natural beauty,

prepare and publish a plan which formulates their policy for the management of the area of outstanding natural beauty and for the carrying out of their functions in relation to it.

(3) Subsection (2) does not apply where, before the end of the period mentioned in that subsection, a conservation board has been established for the area of outstanding natural beauty.

(4) A plan prepared under subsection (1) or (2) is to be known as an area of outstanding natural beauty management plan.

(5) A conservation board or relevant local authority may, instead of preparing a plan under subsection (1) or (2),—

(a) review any plan for the management of the area of outstanding natural beauty which has been prepared before the commencement of this section—

(i) by a local authority, or

(ii) by a joint committee established by two or more local authorities, and

(b) adopt the plan as reviewed as their area of outstanding natural beauty management plan, and

(c) publish it under subsection (1) or (2) within the time required by that subsection.

(6) A conservation board may, within six months of the date on which they are established, adopt an area of outstanding natural beauty management plan prepared for their area of outstanding natural beauty by the relevant local authority as their area of outstanding natural beauty management plan, and publish it under subsection (1).

(7) Subject to subsection (8), a conservation board shall review their area of outstanding natural beauty management plan before the end of the period of five years beginning with the date on which it was published and, after the first review, at intervals of not more than five years.

(8) Where a conservation board have adopted a plan under subsection (6), the first review must take place before the end of the period of three years beginning with the date on which the plan was published.

(9) Where an area of outstanding natural beauty management plan has been prepared under subsection (2), the relevant local authority shall review the plan before the end of the period of five years beginning with the date on which it was published and, after the first review, at intervals of not more than five years, but this subsection does not apply where a conservation board has been established for the area of outstanding natural beauty.

(10) Where a conservation board or relevant local authority review any plan under this section, they shall—

(a) determine on that review whether it would be expedient to amend the plan and what (if any) amendments would be appropriate,

(b) make any amendments that they consider appropriate, and

(c) publish a report on the review specifying any amendments made.

(11) In this section "relevant local authority" means—

(a) in the case of an area of outstanding natural beauty which is wholly comprised in one principal area, the local authority for that area, and

(b) in any other case, the local authorities for all the principal areas wholly or partly comprised in the area of outstanding natural beauty, acting jointly.

Supplementary provisions relating to management plans.

90.—(1) A conservation board or relevant local authority which is proposing to publish, adopt or review any plan under section 89 shall—

(a) give notice of the proposal—

(i) if the area of outstanding natural beauty is in England, to the Agency and English Nature,

(ii) if the area of outstanding natural beauty is in Wales, to the Council, and

(iii) in the case of a conservation board, to every local authority whose area is wholly or partly comprised in the area of outstanding natural beauty,

(b) send a copy of the plan, together (where appropriate) with any proposed amendments of the plan, to every body to which notice of the proposal is required to be given by paragraph (a), and

(c) take into consideration any observations made by any such body.

(2) A conservation board or relevant local authority shall send to the Secretary of State or the National Assembly for Wales a copy of every plan, notice or report which they are required to publish under section 89.

(3) In this section "relevant local authority" has the same meaning as in section 89.

91.—(1) The Secretary of State (as respects England) or the National Assembly for Wales (as respects Wales) may make grants to a conservation board, of such amounts and on such terms and conditions as the Secretary of State or the Assembly thinks fit.

(2) Before determining the amount of any grant which he proposes to make to a conservation board under this section, or the purpose for which the grant is to be made, the Secretary of State shall consult the Agency.

(3) Before determining the amount of any grant which it proposes to make to a conservation board under this section, or the purpose for which the grant is to be made, the National Assembly for Wales shall consult the Council.

Grants to conservation boards.

92.—(1) In this Part, unless a contrary intention appears—

"the 1949 Act" means the National Parks and Access to the Countryside Act 1949;

"the Agency" means the Countryside Agency;

"area of outstanding natural beauty" has the meaning given by section 82(3);

"conservation board" has the meaning given by section 86(1);

"the Council" means the Countryside Council for Wales;

"liability", in relation to the transfer of liabilities from one person to another, does not include criminal liability;

"local authority" means a principal council within the meaning of the Local Government Act 1972;

"principal area" has the same meaning as in the Local Government Act 1972.

Interpretation of Part IV and supplementary provision.
1949 c. 97.

1972 c. 70.

(2) Any reference in this Part to the conservation of the natural beauty of an area includes a reference to the conservation of its flora, fauna and geological and physiographical features.

(3) This Part does not apply in relation to any of the lands mentioned in section 112(1) of the 1949 Act (Epping Forest and Burnham Beeches).

93. Schedule 15 (which contains consequential amendments and transitional provisions relating to areas of outstanding natural beauty) has effect.

Consequential amendments and transitional provisions.

Part V

MISCELLANEOUS AND SUPPLEMENTARY

Local access forums

94.—(1) The appointing authority for any area shall in accordance with regulations establish for that area, or for each part of it, an advisory body to be known as a local access forum.

(2) For the purposes of this section—

(a) the local highway authority is the appointing authority for their area, except any part of it in a National Park, and

(b) the National Park authority for a National Park is the appointing authority for the National Park.

(3) A local access forum consists of members appointed by the appointing authority in accordance with regulations.

(4) It is the function of a local access forum, as respects the area for which it is established, to advise—

(a) the appointing authority,

(b) any body exercising functions under Part I in relation to land in that area,

(c) if the appointing authority is a National Park authority, the local highway authority for any part of that area, and

(d) such other bodies as may be prescribed,

as to the improvement of public access to land in that area for the purposes of open-air recreation and the enjoyment of the area, and as to such other matters as may be prescribed.

(5) The bodies mentioned in paragraphs (a) to (d) of subsection (4) shall have regard, in carrying out their functions, to any relevant advice given to them by a local access forum under that subsection or any other provision of this Act.

(6) In carrying out its functions, a local access forum shall have regard to—

(a) the needs of land management,

(b) the desirability of conserving the natural beauty of the area for which it is established, including the flora, fauna and geological and physiographical features of the area, and

(c) guidance given from time to time by the Secretary of State (as respects England) or the National Assembly for Wales (as respects Wales).

(7) Subsection (1) does not apply to the council of a London borough or to any part of their area unless the council so resolve.

(8) The Secretary of State, as respects England, or the National Assembly for Wales, as respects Wales, if satisfied that no local access forum is required for any area or part of any area, may direct that subsection (1) is not to apply in relation to that area or part.

(9) Before giving a direction under subsection (8) as respects an area or part of an area, the Secretary of State or the National Assembly for Wales must consult the appointing authority for the area and the appropriate countryside body.

(10) In this section—

"appropriate countryside body" has the same meaning as in Part I;

"local highway authority" has the same meaning as in the 1980 Act;

"prescribed" means prescribed by regulations;

"regulations" means regulations made, as respects England, by the Secretary of State, and, as respects Wales, by the National Assembly for Wales.

95.—(1) Regulations under section 94 may in particular include provision—   Local access forums: supplementary.

    (a) as to the appointment as members of a local access forum of persons appearing to the appointing authority to be representative of persons of any specified description or of any specified body;

    (b) as to the establishment by appointing authorities of joint local access forums.

(2) The regulations must provide for the appointment of persons appearing to the appointing authority to be representative of—

    (a) users of local rights of way or the right conferred by section 2(1);

    (b) owners and occupiers of access land or land over which local rights of way subsist;

    (c) any other interests especially relevant to the authority's area.

(3) In subsection (2)—

"access land" has the same meaning as in Part I;

"local rights of way" has the meaning given by section 60(5), but as if the references there to a local highway authority and their area were references to an appointing authority and their area.

(4) The Secretary of State and the National Assembly for Wales, in making regulations under section 94 containing such provision as is mentioned in subsection (2), must have regard to the desirability of maintaining a reasonable balance between the number of members of any local access forum appointed in accordance with paragraph (a) and in accordance with paragraph (b) of subsection (2).

(5) Regulations under section 94 may include such supplementary or incidental provision as appears to the Secretary of State or National Assembly for Wales (as the case may be) to be necessary or expedient.

(6) For the purposes of section 94, the Broads are to be treated as a National Park and the Broads Authority as a National Park authority.

(7) In subsection (6) "the Broads" has the same meaning as in the Norfolk and Suffolk Broads Act 1988.   1988 c. 4.

(8) Regulations under section 94 shall be made by statutory instrument, and a statutory instrument containing such regulations made by the Secretary of State shall be subject to annulment in pursuance of a resolution of either House of Parliament.

PART V

Management agreements

Management
agreements.

96. In section 39 of the 1981 Act (management agreements with owners and occupiers of land)—

(a) in subsection (1) the words "both in the countryside and" are omitted, and

(b) at the end of subsection (5) (authorities which may enter into management agreements) there is inserted—

"(d) as respects any land in England, the Countryside Agency;

(e) as respects any land in Wales, the Countryside Council for Wales;

(f) as respects land in any area of outstanding natural beauty designated under section 82 of the Countryside and Rights of Way Act 2000 for which a conservation board has been established under section 86 of that Act, that board."

Norfolk and Suffolk Broads

Duty of public
bodies etc.
regarding the
Broads.
1988 c. 4.

97. In Part IV of the Norfolk and Suffolk Broads Act 1988, before section 18 there is inserted—

"General duty of
public bodies
etc.

17A.—(1) In exercising or performing any functions in relation to, or so as to affect, land in the Broads, a relevant authority shall have regard to the purposes of—

(a) conserving and enhancing the natural beauty of the Broads;

(b) promoting the enjoyment of the Broads by the public; and

(c) protecting the interests of navigation.

(2) The following are relevant authorities for the purposes of this section—

(a) any Minister of the Crown,

(b) any public body,

(c) any statutory undertaker,

(d) any person holding public office.

(3) In subsection (2)—

"public body" includes

(a) a county council, district council or parish council;

1990 c. 8.

(b) a joint planning board within the meaning of section 2 of the Town and Country Planning Act 1990;

1972 c. 70.

(c) a joint committee appointed under section 102(1)(b) of the Local Government Act 1972;

"public office" means—

(a) an office under Her Majesty;

(b) an office created or continued in existence by a public general Act; or

(c) an office the remuneration in respect of which is paid out of money provided by Parliament."

Town and village greens

98.—(1) Section 22 of the Commons Registration Act 1965 (interpretation) is amended as follows.

Registration of town and village greens.
1965 c. 64.

(2) In subsection (1), in the definition of "town or village green" for the words after "lawful sports and pastimes" there is substituted "or which falls within subsection (1A) of this section.

(3) After that subsection there is inserted—

"(1A) Land falls within this subsection if it is land on which for not less than twenty years a significant number of the inhabitants of any locality, or of any neighbourhood within a locality, have indulged in lawful sports and pastimes as of right, and either—

(a) continue to do so, or

(b) have ceased to do so for not more than such period as may be prescribed, or determined in accordance with prescribed provisions.

(1B) If regulations made for the purposes of paragraph (b) of subsection (1A) of this section provide for the period mentioned in that paragraph to come to an end unless prescribed steps are taken, the regulations may also require registration authorities to make available in accordance with the regulations, on payment of any prescribed fee, information relating to the taking of any such steps.".

Supplementary

99.—(1) In Schedule 1 to the National Assembly for Wales (Transfer of Functions) Order 1999—

Wales.
S.I. 1999/672.

(a) the reference to the 1980 Act is to be treated as referring to that Act as amended by this Act, and

(b) the reference to the 1981 Act is to be treated as referring to that Act as amended by this Act.

(2) In that Schedule, at the end of the list of Public General Acts there is inserted—

" **Countryside and Rights of Way Act 2000 (c. 37)** Schedule 11.".

(3) Subsection (1), and the amendment made by subsection (2), do not affect the power to make further Orders varying or omitting the references mentioned in subsection (1) or the provision inserted by subsection (2).

100.—(1) Subject to the provisions of any order under this section, the following provisions of this Act do not apply in relation to the Isles of Scilly—

Isles of Scilly.

(a) Part I; and

(b) sections 58 to 61 and 71.

(2) The Secretary of State may by order made by statutory instrument provide for the application of any of the provisions mentioned in subsection (1) in relation to the Isles of Scilly, subject to such modifications as may be specified in the order.

PART V

(3) Part IV applies in relation to the Isles of Scilly subject to such modifications as may be specified in an order made by the Secretary of State by statutory instrument.

(4) Before making an order under subsection (2) or (3), the Secretary of State shall consult the Council of the Isles of Scilly.

(5) In section 344 of the 1980 Act (application to the Isles of Scilly)—

    (a) in subsection (2)(a) for "121" there is substituted "121E, 130A to 130D", and

    (b) before "146" there is inserted "137ZA(4)".

Expenses.

101. There shall be paid out of money provided by Parliament—

    (a) any increase attributable to this Act in the sums required by the Secretary of State for making grants to the Countryside Agency or English Nature,

    (b) any administrative expenses of a Minister of the Crown which are attributable to this Act,

    (c) any other expenditure of a Minister of the Crown or government department which is attributable to this Act,

    (d) any increase attributable to this Act in the sums which under any other enactment are payable out of money so provided.

Repeals.

102. The enactments mentioned in Schedule 16 are repealed to the extent specified.

Commencement.

103.—(1) The following provisions of this Act come into force on the day on which this Act is passed—

    section 81(2) and (3),

    this section, and

    section 104.

(2) The following provisions of this Act come into force at the end of the period of two months beginning with the day on which this Act is passed—

    section 1 and Schedule 1,

    sections 3 to 11 and Schedule 3,

    sections 15 to 17,

    section 19,

    Chapters II and III of Part I,

    sections 40 to 45,

    section 52,

    sections 58 and 59,

    sections 64 to 67 and Schedule 7 (apart from paragraphs 6 and 7 of that Schedule),

    Part III (apart from section 81(2) and (3)), and Schedules 8, 9, 10, 11 and 12 and Parts III and IV of Schedule 16,

    sections 94 and 95, and

    section 98.

(3) The remaining provisions of this Act come into force on such day as the Secretary of State (as respects England) or the National Assembly for Wales (as respects Wales) may by order made by statutory instrument appoint.

(4) Different days may be appointed under subsection (3) for different purposes or different areas.

(5) An order under subsection (3) may contain such transitional provisions or savings (including provisions modifying the effect of any enactment) as appear to the Secretary of State or the National Assembly for Wales (as the case may be) to be necessary or expedient in connection with any provision brought into force by the order.

104.—(1) In this Act—

    "the 1980 Act" means the Highways Act 1980;

    "the 1981 Act" means the Wildlife and Countryside Act 1981;

    "local access forum" means a local access forum established under section 94.

Interpretation, short title and extent.

1980 c. 66.
1981 c. 69.

(2) Any reference in this Act, or in any enactment amended by this Act, to the commencement of any provision of this Act is, in relation to any area, a reference to the commencement of that provision in relation to that area.

(3) This Act may be cited as the Countryside and Rights of Way Act 2000.

(4) Subject to the following provisions of this section, this Act extends to England and Wales only.

(5) The following provisions extend also to Scotland—

    sections 67 and 76;

    in Schedule 7, paragraphs 3 and 5 to 7;

    in Schedule 10, paragraph 2.

(6) Paragraph 1 of Schedule 10 extends to Scotland only.

(7) The provisions of Schedule 8 and of so much of Part III of Schedule 16 as relates to the enactments referred to in paragraphs 2 and 3 of Schedule 8 have the same extent as the enactments which they amend or repeal.

SCHEDULES

Section 1(2).

SCHEDULE 1

EXCEPTED LAND FOR PURPOSES OF PART I

PART I

EXCEPTED LAND

1. Land on which the soil is being, or has at any time within the previous twelve months been, disturbed by any ploughing or drilling undertaken for the purposes of planting or sowing crops or trees.

2. Land covered by buildings or the curtilage of such land.

3. Land within 20 metres of a dwelling.

4. Land used as a park or garden.

5. Land used for the getting of minerals by surface working (including quarrying).

6. Land used for the purposes of a railway (including a light railway) or tramway.

7. Land used for the purposes of a golf course, racecourse or aerodrome.

8. Land which does not fall within any of the preceding paragraphs and is covered by works used for the purposes of a statutory undertaking or a telecommunications code system, or the curtilage of any such land.

9. Land as respects which development which will result in the land becoming land falling within any of paragraphs 2 to 8 is in the course of being carried out.

10. Land within 20 metres of a building which is used for housing livestock, not being a temporary or moveable structure.

11. Land covered by pens in use for the temporary reception or detention of livestock.

12. Land habitually used for the training of racehorses.

1892 c. 43.
1900 c. 56.

13. Land the use of which is regulated by byelaws under section 14 of the Military Lands Act 1892 or section 2 of the Military Lands Act 1900.

PART II

SUPPLEMENTARY PROVISIONS

14. In this Schedule—

"building" includes any structure or erection and any part of a building as so defined, but does not include any fence or wall, or anything which is a means of access as defined by section 34; and for this purpose "structure" includes any tent, caravan or other temporary or moveable structure;

1990 c. 8.

"development" and "minerals" have the same meaning as in the Town and Country Planning Act 1990;

"ploughing" and "drilling" include respectively agricultural or forestry operations similar to ploughing and agricultural or forestry operations similar to drilling;

"statutory undertaker" means—

(a) a person authorised by any enactment to carry on any railway, light railway, tramway, road transport, water transport, canal, inland navigation, dock, harbour, pier or lighthouse undertaking or any undertaking for the supply of hydraulic power,

(b) any public gas transporter, within the meaning of Part I of the Gas Act 1986,

1986 c. 44.

(c) any water or sewerage undertaker,

(d) any holder of a licence under section 6(1) of the Electricity Act 1989, or

1989 c. 29.

(e) the Environment Agency, the Post Office or the Civil Aviation Authority;

"statutory undertaking" means—

(a) the undertaking of a statutory undertaker, or

(b) an airport to which Part V of the Airports Act 1986 applies.

1986 c. 31.

15.—(1) Land is not to be treated as excepted land by reason of any development carried out on the land, if the carrying out of the development requires planning permission under Part III of the Town and Country Planning Act 1990 and that permission has not been granted.

1990 c. 8.

(2) Sub-paragraph (1) does not apply where the development is treated by section 191(2) of the Town and Country Planning Act 1990 as being lawful for the purposes of that Act.

16. The land which is excepted land by virtue of paragraph 10 does not include—

(a) any means of access, as defined by section 34, or

(b) any way leading to such a means of access,

if the means of access is necessary for giving the public reasonable access to access land.

17. Land which is habitually used for the training of racehorses is not to be treated by virtue of paragraph 11 as excepted land except—

(a) between dawn and midday on any day, and

(b) at any other time when it is in use for that purpose.

SCHEDULE 2

Section 2.

RESTRICTIONS TO BE OBSERVED BY PERSONS EXERCISING RIGHT OF ACCESS

General restrictions

1. Section 2(1) does not entitle a person to be on any land if, in or on that land, he—

(a) drives or rides any vehicle other than an invalid carriage as defined by section 20(2) of the Chronically Sick and Disabled Persons Act 1970,

1970 c. 44.

(b) uses a vessel or sailboard on any non-tidal water,

(c) has with him any animal other than a dog,

(d) commits any criminal offence,

(e) lights or tends a fire or does any act which is likely to cause a fire,

(f) intentionally or recklessly takes, kills, injures or disturbs any animal, bird or fish,

(g) intentionally or recklessly takes, damages or destroys any eggs or nests,

(h) feeds any livestock,

(i) bathes in any non-tidal water,

(j) engages in any operations of or connected with hunting, shooting, fishing, trapping, snaring, taking or destroying of animals, birds or fish or has with him any engine, instrument or apparatus used for hunting, shooting, fishing, trapping, snaring, taking or destroying animals, birds or fish,

(k) uses or has with him any metal detector,

(l) intentionally removes, damages or destroys any plant, shrub, tree or root or any part of a plant, shrub, tree or root,

(m) obstructs the flow of any drain or watercourse, or opens, shuts or otherwise interferes with any sluice-gate or other apparatus,

(n) without reasonable excuse, interferes with any fence, barrier or other device designed to prevent accidents to people or to enclose livestock,

(o) neglects to shut any gate or to fasten it where any means of doing so is provided, except where it is reasonable to assume that a gate is intended to be left open,

(p) affixes or writes any advertisement, bill, placard or notice,

(q) in relation to any lawful activity which persons are engaging in or are about to engage in on that or adjoining land, does anything which is intended by him to have the effect—

    (i) of intimidating those persons so as to deter them or any of them from engaging in that activity,

    (ii) of obstructing that activity, or

    (iii) of disrupting that activity,

(r) without reasonable excuse, does anything which (whether or not intended by him to have the effect mentioned in paragraph (q)) disturbs, annoys or obstructs any persons engaged in a lawful activity on the land,

(s) engages in any organised games, or in camping, hang-gliding or para-gliding, or

(t) engages in any activity which is organised or undertaken (whether by him or another) for any commercial purpose.

2.—(1) In paragraph 1(k), "metal detector" means any device designed or adapted for detecting or locating any metal or mineral in the ground.

(2) For the purposes of paragraph 1(q) and (r), activity on any occasion on the part of a person or persons on land is "lawful" if he or they may engage in the activity on the land on that occasion without committing an offence or trespassing on the land.

3. Regulations may amend paragraphs 1 and 2.

4. During the period beginning with 1st March and ending with 31st July in each year, section 2(1) does not entitle a person to be on any land if he takes, or allows to enter or remain, any dog which is not on a short lead.

5. Whatever the time of year, section 2(1) does not entitle a person to be on any land if he takes, or allows to enter or remain, any dog which is not on a short lead and which is in the vicinity of livestock.

6. In paragraphs 4 and 5, "short lead" means a lead of fixed length and of not more than two metres.

Removal or relaxation of restrictions

7.—(1) The relevant authority may by direction, with the consent of the owner of any land, remove or relax any of the restrictions imposed by paragraphs 1, 4 and 5 in relation to that land, either indefinitely or during a specified period.

(2) In sub-paragraph (1), the reference to a specified period includes references—

(a) to a specified period in every calendar year, or

(b) to a period which is to be determined by the owner of the land in accordance with the direction and notified by him to the relevant authority in accordance with regulations.

(3) Regulations may make provision as to—

(a) the giving or revocation of directions under this paragraph,

(b) the variation of any direction given under this paragraph by a subsequent direction so given,

(c) the giving or revocation of consent for the purposes of sub-paragraph (1), and

(d) the steps to be taken by the relevant authority or the owner for informing the public about any direction under this paragraph or its revocation.

(4) In this paragraph—

"the relevant authority" has the meaning given by section 21;

"owner", in relation to any land which is subject to a farm business tenancy within the meaning of the Agricultural Tenancies Act 1995 or a tenancy 1995 c. 8. to which the Agricultural Holdings Act 1986 applies, means the tenant 1986 c. 5. under that tenancy.

Dedicated land

8. In relation to land to which a dedication under section 16 relates (whether or not it would be access land apart from the dedication), the provisions of this Schedule have effect subject to the terms of the dedication.

SCHEDULE 3   Section 8(2).

DELEGATION OF APPELLATE FUNCTIONS

Interpretation

1. In this Schedule—

"appointed person" means a person appointed under section 8(1)(a);

"the appointing authority" means—

(a) the Secretary of State, in relation to an appointment made by him, or

(b) the National Assembly for Wales, in relation to an appointment made by it;

"appointment", in the case of any appointed person, means appointment under section 8(1)(a).

SCH. 3

Appointments

2. An appointment under section 8(1)(a) must be in writing and—

    (a) may relate to any particular appeal or matter specified in the appointment or to appeals or matters of a description so specified,

    (b) may provide for any function to which it relates to be exercisable by the appointed person either unconditionally or subject to the fulfilment of such conditions as may be specified in the appointment, and

    (c) may, by notice in writing given to the appointed person, be revoked at any time by the appointing authority in respect of any appeal or matter which has not been determined by the appointed person before that time.

Powers of appointed person

3. Subject to the provisions of this Schedule, an appointed person shall, in relation to any appeal or matter to which his appointment relates, have the same powers and duties as the appointing authority, other than—

    (a) any function of making regulations;

    (b) any function of holding an inquiry or other hearing or of causing an inquiry or other hearing to be held; or

    (c) any function of appointing a person for the purpose—

        (i) of enabling persons to appear before and be heard by the person so appointed; or

        (ii) of referring any question or matter to that person.

Holding of local inquiries and other hearings by appointed persons

4.—(1) If either of the parties to an appeal or matter expresses a wish to appear before and be heard by the appointed person, the appointed person shall give both of them an opportunity of appearing and being heard.

(2) Whether or not a party to an appeal or matter has asked for an opportunity to appear and be heard, the appointed person—

    (a) may hold a local inquiry or other hearing in connection with the appeal or matter, and

    (b) shall, if the appointing authority so directs, hold a local inquiry in connection with the appeal or matter.

(3) Where an appointed person holds a local inquiry or other hearing by virtue of this Schedule, an assessor may be appointed by the appointing authority to sit with the appointed person at the inquiry or hearing and advise him on any matters arising, notwithstanding that the appointed person is to determine the appeal or matter.

(4) Subject to paragraph 5, the costs of a local inquiry held under this Schedule shall be defrayed by the appointing authority.

Local inquiries under this Schedule: evidence and costs

1972 c. 70.

5. Subsections (2) to (5) of section 250 of the Local Government Act 1972 (local inquiries: evidence and costs) shall apply to local inquiries or other hearings held under this Schedule by an appointed person as they apply to inquiries caused to be held under that section by a Minister, but as if—

    (a) in subsection (2) (evidence) the reference to the person appointed to hold the inquiry were a reference to the appointed person,

    (b) in subsection (4) (recovery of costs of holding the inquiry)—

        (i) references to the Minister causing the inquiry to be held were references to the appointing authority, and

(ii) references to a local authority included references to the appropriate countryside body, and

(c) in subsection (5) (orders as to the costs of the parties) the reference to the Minister causing the inquiry to be held were a reference to the appointed person or the appointing authority.

Revocation of appointments and making of new appointments

6.—(1) Where under paragraph 2(c) the appointment of the appointed person is revoked in respect of any appeal or matter, the appointing authority shall, unless he proposes to determine the appeal or matter himself, appoint another person under section 8(1)(a) to determine the appeal or matter instead.

(2) Where such a new appointment is made, the consideration of the appeal or matter, or any hearing in connection with it, shall be begun afresh.

(3) Nothing in sub-paragraph (2) shall require any person to be given an opportunity of making fresh representations or modifying or withdrawing any representations already made.

Certain acts and omissions of appointed person to be treated as those of appointing authority

7.—(1) Anything done or omitted to be done by an appointed person in, or in connection with, the exercise or purported exercise of any function to which the appointment relates shall be treated for all purposes as done or omitted to be done by the appointing authority.

(2) Sub-paragraph (1) does not apply—

(a) for the purposes of so much of any contract made between the appointing authority and the appointed person as relates to the exercise of the function, or

(b) for the purposes of any criminal proceedings brought in respect of anything done or omitted to be done as mentioned in that sub-paragraph.

SCHEDULE 4

MINOR AND CONSEQUENTIAL AMENDMENTS RELATING TO PART I

Law of Property Act 1925 (c. 20)

1. In section 193(1) of the Law of Property Act 1925 (rights of public over commons and waste lands), in paragraph (b) of the proviso, after "injuriously affected," there is inserted "for conserving flora, fauna or geological or physiographical features of the land,".

Forestry Act 1967 (c. 10)

2. In section 9 of the Forestry Act 1967 (requirement of licence for felling), in the definition of "public open space" in subsection (6), after "1949" there is inserted "or Part I of the Countryside and Rights of Way Act 2000)".

Agriculture Act 1967 (c. 52)

3. In section 52 of the Agriculture Act 1967 (control of afforestation), in the definition of "public open space" in subsection (15), after "1949" there is inserted "or Part I of the Countryside and Rights of Way Act 2000)".

SCH. 4

Countryside Act 1968 (c. 41)

4. In section 2(6) of the Countryside Act 1968 (Countryside Agency and Countryside Council for Wales to make recommendations to public bodies in relation to byelaws) for "and the Act of 1949" there is substituted ", the Act of 1949 and Part I of the Countryside and Rights of Way Act 2000".

Local Government Act 1974 (c. 7)

5. In section 9 of the Local Government Act 1974 (grants and loans by Countryside Agency and Countryside Council for Wales), for "or the National Parks and Access to the Countryside Act 1949" there is substituted ", the National Parks and Access to the Countryside Act 1949 or the Countryside and Rights of Way Act 2000".

Wildlife and Countryside Act 1981 (c. 69)

6. In paragraph 13(1) of Schedule 13 to the Wildlife and Countryside Act 1981 (Countryside Agency's annual report on the discharge of their functions) after "1968 Act" there is inserted ", the Countryside and Rights of Way Act 2000".

Section 51.

SCHEDULE 5

DEFINITIVE MAPS AND STATEMENTS AND RESTRICTED BYWAYS

PART I

AMENDMENTS OF PART III OF WILDLIFE AND COUNTRYSIDE ACT 1981

1.—(1) Section 53 of the 1981 Act is amended as follows.

(2) In subsection (1) (meaning of "definitive map and statement") after "subject to section 57(3)" there is inserted "and 57A(1)".

(3) In subsection (3)(a)(iii), after "public path" there is inserted "or a restricted byway".

(4) In subsection (3)(c)(i) for "a right of way to which this Part applies" there is substituted "a right of way such that the land over which the right subsists is a public path or, subject to section 54A, a byway open to all traffic".

(5) In subsection (4), after "public path" there is inserted ", restricted byway".

(6) After subsection (4) there is inserted—

"(4A) Subsection (4B) applies to evidence which, when considered with all other relevant evidence available to the surveying authority, shows as respects a way shown in a definitive map and statement as a restricted byway that the public have, and had immediately before the commencement of section 47 of the Countryside and Rights of Way Act 2000, a right of way for vehicular and all other kinds of traffic over that way.

(4B) For the purposes of subsection (3)(c)(ii), such evidence is evidence which, when so considered, shows that the way concerned ought, subject to section 54A, to be shown in the definitive map and statement as a byway open to all traffic."

(7) After subsection (5) there is inserted—

"(5A) Evidence to which subsection (4B) applies on the commencement of section 47 of the Countryside and Rights of Way Act 2000 shall for the purposes of subsection (5) and any application made under it be treated as not having been discovered by the surveying authority before the commencement of that section."

2. After section 53 of that Act there is inserted—

"Power to include modifications in other orders.

53A.—(1) This section applies to any order—

(a) which is of a description prescribed by regulations made by the Secretary of State,

(b) whose coming into operation would, as regards any definitive map and statement, be an event within section 53(3)(a),

(c) which is made by the surveying authority, and

(d) which does not affect land outside the authority's area.

(2) The authority may include in the order such provision as it would be required to make under section 53(2)(b) in consequence of the coming into operation of the other provisions of the order.

(3) An authority which has included any provision in an order by virtue of subsection (2)—

(a) may at any time before the order comes into operation, and

(b) shall, if the order becomes subject to special parliamentary procedure,

withdraw the order and substitute for it an order otherwise identical but omitting any provision so included.

(4) Anything done for the purposes of any enactment in relation to an order withdrawn under subsection (3) shall be treated for those purposes as done in relation to the substituted order.

(5) No requirement for the confirmation of an order applies to provisions included in the order by virtue of subsection (2), but any power to modify an order includes power to make consequential modifications to any provision so included.

(6) Provisions included in an order by virtue of subsection (2) shall take effect on the date specified under section 56(3A) as the relevant date.

(7) Where any enactment provides for questioning the validity of an order on any grounds, the validity of any provision included by virtue of subsection (2) may be questioned in the same way on the grounds—

(a) that it is not within the powers of this Part, or

(b) that any requirement of this Part or of regulations made under it has not been complied with.

(8) Subject to subsections (5) to (7), the Secretary of State may by regulations provide that any procedural requirement as to the making or coming into operation of an order to which this section applies shall not apply, or shall apply with modifications prescribed by the regulations, to so much of the order as contains provision included by virtue of subsection (2).

(9) Regulations under this section shall be made by statutory instrument which shall be subject to annulment in pursuance of a resolution of either House of Parliament.

Register of applications under section 53.

53B.—(1) Every surveying authority shall keep, in such manner as may be prescribed, a register containing such information as may be prescribed with respect to applications under section 53(5).

(2) The register shall contain such information as may be prescribed with respect to the manner in which such applications have been dealt with.

(3) Regulations may make provision for the register to be kept in two or more parts, each part containing such information relating to applications under section 53(5) as may be prescribed.

(4) Regulations may make provision—

(a) for a specified part of the register to contain copies of applications and of the maps submitted with them, and

(b) for the entry relating to any application, and everything relating to it, to be removed from any part of the register when—

(i) the application (including any appeal to the Secretary of State) has been finally disposed of, and

(ii) if an order is made, a decision has been made to confirm or not to confirm the order,

(without prejudice to the inclusion of any different entry relating to it in another part of the register).

(5) Every register kept under this section shall be available for inspection free of charge at all reasonable hours.

(6) In this section—

"prescribed" means prescribed by regulations;

"regulations" means regulations made by the Secretary of State by statutory instrument;

and a statutory instrument containing regulations under this section shall be subject to annulment in pursuance of a resolution of either House of Parliament."

3.—(1) Until the coming into force of section 47(1) of this Act, section 54 of the 1981 Act (duty to reclassify roads used as public paths) has effect as follows.

(2) In subsection (2)—

(a) for the words from the beginning to "by" there is substituted "Where the particulars relating to any road used as a public path have been reviewed under subsection (1)(a), the definitive map and statement shall be modified so as to show that way by", and

(b) the words from "and shall not" to the end are omitted.

(3) In subsection (3), for the words "A road used as a public path" there is substituted "Such a way".

(4) After subsection (5) there is inserted—

"(5A) No order under this Part modifying a definitive map and statement, and no provision included by virtue of section 53A(2) in any order, shall use the expression "road used as a public path" to describe any way not already shown as such in the map and statement."

4. After section 54 of that Act there is inserted—

"BOATs not to be added to definitive maps.

54A.—(1) No order under this Part shall, after the cut-off date, modify a definitive map and statement so as to show as a byway open to all traffic any way not shown in the map and statement as a highway of any description.

(2) In this section "the cut-off date" means, subject to regulations under subsection (3), 1st January 2026.

(3) The Secretary of State may make regulations—

(a) substituting as the cut-off date a date later than the date specified in subsection (2) or for the time being substituted under this paragraph;

(b) containing such transitional provisions or savings as appear to the Secretary of State to be necessary or expedient in connection with the operation of subsection (1), including in particular its operation in relation to—

(i) an order under section 53(2) for which on the cut-off date an application is pending,

(ii) an order under this Part which on that date has been made but not confirmed,

(iii) an order under section 55 made after that date, or

(iv) an order under this Part relating to any way as respects which such an order, or any provision of such an order, has after that date been to any extent quashed.

(4) Regulations under subsection (3)(a)—

(a) may specify different dates for different areas; but

(b) may not specify a date later than 1st January 2031, except as respects an area within subsection (5).

(5) An area is within this subsection if it is in—

(a) the Isles of Scilly, or

(b) an area which, at any time before the repeal by section 73 of this Act of sections 27 to 34 of the 1949 Act—

(i) was excluded from the operation of those sections by virtue of any provision of the 1949 Act, or

(ii) would have been so excluded but for a resolution having effect under section 35(2) of that Act.

(6) Where by virtue of regulations under subsection (3) there are different cut-off dates for areas into which different parts of any way extend, the cut-off date in relation to that way is the later or latest of those dates.

(7) Where it appears to the Secretary of State that any provision of this Part can by virtue of subsection (1) have no further application he may by order make such amendments or repeals in this Part as appear to him to be, in consequence, necessary or expedient.

(8) An order or regulations under this section shall be made by statutory instrument which shall be subject to annulment in pursuance of a resolution of either House of Parliament."

5. In section 55 of that Act (no further surveys or reviews under the National   1949 c. 97. Parks and Access to the Countryside Act 1949), after subsection (6) there is inserted—

"(7) Every way which—

SCH. 5

　　(a) in pursuance of an order under subsection (5) is shown in a definitive map and statement as a byway open to all traffic, a bridleway or a footpath, and

　　(b) before the making of the order, was shown in the map and statement under review as a road used as a public path,

shall be a highway maintainable at the public expense.

　　(8) Subsection (7) does not oblige a highway authority to provide, on a way shown in a definitive map and statement as a byway open to all traffic, a metalled carriage-way or a carriage-way which is by any other means provided with a surface suitable for the passage of vehicles."

　　6.—(1) Section 56 of that Act (effect of definitive map and statement) is amended as follows.

　　(2) In subsection (1)(d)—

　　(a) for "road used as a public path" there is substituted "restricted byway",

　　(b) after "the map shall" there is inserted ", subject to subsection (2A),", and

　　(c) after "leading a horse" there is inserted "together with a right of way for vehicles other than mechanically propelled vehicles".

　　(3) After subsection (1) there is inserted—

1988 c. 52.

　　"(1A) In subsection (1)(d) "mechanically propelled vehicle" does not include an electrically assisted pedal cycle of a class prescribed for the purposes of section 189(1)(c) of the Road Traffic Act 1988."

　　(4) In subsection (2)—

　　(a) in paragraph (a)—

　　　　(i) after "this Part" there is inserted "or an order to which section 53A applies which includes provision made by virtue of subsection (2) of that section", and

　　　　(ii) after "means" there is inserted ", subject to subsection (2A)," and

　　(b) in paragraph (b), after "(3)" there is inserted "or (3A)".

　　(5) After that subsection there is inserted—

　　"(2A) In the case of a map prepared before the date of the coming into force of section 47 of the Countryside and Rights of Way Act 2000—

　　(a) subsection (1)(d) and (e) have effect subject to the operation of any enactment or instrument, and to any other event, whereby a way shown on the map as a restricted byway has, on or before that date—

　　　　(i) been authorised to be stopped up, diverted or widened, or

　　　　(ii) become a public path, and

　　(b) subsection (2)(a) has effect in relation to any way so shown with the substitution of that date for the date mentioned there."

　　(6) After subsection (3) there is inserted—

　　"(3A) Every order to which section 53A applies which includes provision made by virtue of subsection (2) of that section shall specify, as the relevant date for the purposes of the order, such date as the authority may in accordance with regulations made by the Secretary of State determine."

　　(7) After subsection (4) there is inserted—

"(4A) Regulations under this section shall be made by statutory instrument which shall be subject to annulment in pursuance of a resolution of either House of Parliament."

(8) Subsection (5) is omitted.

7.—(1) Section 57 of that Act (supplementary provisions as to definitive maps and statements) is amended as follows.

(2) In subsection (1), the words "on such scale as may be so prescribed," are omitted.

(3) In subsection (2), for "section 55(3)" there is substituted "subsection (1) or any other provision of this Part".

(4) In subsection (3) after "for the purposes of the foregoing provisions of this Part" there is inserted ", and for the purposes of section 57A(1),".

(5) After that subsection there is inserted—

"(3A) Where as respects any definitive map and statement the requirements of section 53(2), and of section 55 so far as it applies, have been complied with, the map and statement are to be regarded for the purposes of subsection (3) as having been modified in accordance with the foregoing provisions of this Part whether or not, as respects the map and statement, the requirements of section 54 have been complied with."

(6) After subsection (6) there is inserted—

"(6A) In subsection (1), the reference to an order under the foregoing provisions of this Part includes a reference to so much of an order to which section 53A applies as contains provision made by virtue of subsection (2) of that section; and subsections (5) and (6) apply to—

(a) orders to which section 53A applies modifying the map and statement, and

(b) such documents relating to them as may be prescribed by regulations made by the Secretary of State,

as those subsections apply to orders under this Part modifying the map and statement.

(6B) Regulations under paragraph (b) of subsection (6A) may require any document to be prepared by a surveying authority for the purposes of that paragraph, and any such document shall be in such form as may be prescribed by the regulations.

(6C) Regulations made by the Secretary of State may require any surveying authority—

(a) to keep such other documents as may be prescribed by the regulations available for inspection at such times and places and in such manner as may be so prescribed, or

(b) to provide to any other surveying authority any document so prescribed which that authority is, by regulations under paragraph (a), required to keep available for inspection."

8. After section 57 of that Act there is inserted—

"Consolidation of definitive maps and statements.   57A.—(1) Where—

(a) different definitive maps and statements relate to different parts of a surveying authority's area,

(b) as respects so much of each definitive map and statement as relates to that area the requirements of section 53(2), and of section 55 so far as it applies, have been complied with, and

> (c) there is no part of that area to which no definitive map and statement relate,

the authority may, if it appears to them expedient to do so, prepare a map and statement comprising copies of so much of each definitive map and statement as relates to the authority's area; and where they do so the map and statement so prepared and not, so far as copied, the earlier maps and statements shall be regarded for the purposes of sections 53 to 56 and 57(2) and (3) as the definitive map and statement for the area to which they relate.

(2) The power conferred by subsection (1) is not exercisable by a surveying authority if the definitive map and statement relating to any part of the authority's area is a map and statement in respect of which a review under section 33 of the 1949 Act was begun before the commencement date but has been neither abandoned in pursuance of a direction under section 55(1) nor completed.

(3) References in subsection (1) to a definitive map and statement are, in the case of a map and statement modified in accordance with any of the foregoing provisions of this Part, references to the map and statement as modified.

(4) The statement prepared under subsection (1) shall specify, as the relevant date for the purposes of the map, such date, not being earlier than six months before the preparation of the map and statement, as the authority may determine.

(5) Every surveying authority shall take such steps as they consider expedient for bringing to the attention of the public the preparation by them of any map and statement under subsection (1)."

9. In section 66(1) of that Act (interpretation of Part III) after the definition of "public path" there is inserted—

"restricted byway" has the same meaning as in Part II of the Countryside and Rights of Way Act 2000;".

10. In Schedule 14 to that Act (applications for certain orders under Part III), in paragraph 4(2) at the end there is inserted "(which may include a direction as to the time within which an order is to be made)"

11.—(1) Schedule 15 to that Act (procedure in connection with certain orders) is amended as follows.

(2) In paragraph 3, in sub-paragraph (1)(c) after "order" there is inserted ", which must include particulars of the grounds relied on,".

(3) In sub-paragraph (9) of that paragraph—

(a) after "sub-paragraph" there is inserted "(1)(c) or", and

(b) after "limiting" there is inserted "the grounds which may be relied on or".

(4) In paragraph 7, in sub-paragraph (2) after "shall" there is inserted ", subject to sub-paragraph (2A),".

(5) After sub-paragraph (2) of that paragraph there is inserted—

"(2A) The Secretary of State may, but need not, act as mentioned in sub-paragraph (2)(a) or (b) if, in his opinion, no representation or objection which has been duly made and not withdrawn relates to an issue which would be relevant in determining whether or not to confirm the order, either with or without modifications."

(6) In sub-paragraph (3) of that paragraph, for "the person appointed to hold the inquiry" there is substituted "any person appointed to hold an inquiry".

(7) In paragraph 8—

(a) in sub-paragraph (2)(a) after "the proposal" there is inserted ", which must include particulars of the grounds relied on,",

(b) for sub-paragraph (2)(b) and (c) there is substituted—

"(b) if any representation or objection duly made is not withdrawn (but subject to sub-paragraph (3)), hold a local inquiry or afford any person by whom any such representation or objection has been made an opportunity of being heard by a person appointed by the Secretary of State for the purpose; and

(c) consider the report of any person appointed to hold an inquiry or to hear representations or objections.

(3) The Secretary of State may, but need not, act as mentioned in sub-paragraph (2)(b) if, in his opinion, no representation or objection which has been duly made and not withdrawn relates to an issue which would be relevant in determining whether or not to confirm the order in accordance with his proposal.

(4) Sub-paragraph (2)(a) shall not be construed as limiting the grounds which may be relied on at any local inquiry or hearing held under this paragraph."

(8) Paragraph 9 is omitted and after paragraph 10 there is inserted—

"Hearings and local inquiries

10A.—(1) Subject to sub-paragraph (2), subsections (2) to (5) of section 250 of the Local Government Act 1972 (giving of evidence at, and defraying of costs of, inquiries) shall apply in relation to any hearing or local inquiry held under paragraph 7 or 8 as they apply in relation to a local inquiry which a Minister causes to be held under subsection (1) of that section.   1970 c. 70.

(2) In its application to a hearing or inquiry held under paragraph 7 or 8 by a person appointed under paragraph 10(1), subsection (5) of that section shall have effect as if the reference to the Minister causing the inquiry to be held were a reference to the person so appointed or the Secretary of State.

(3) Section 322A of the Town and Country Planning Act 1990 (orders as to costs where no hearing or inquiry takes place) shall apply in relation to a hearing or local inquiry under paragraph 7 or 8 as it applies in relation to a hearing or local inquiry for the purposes referred to in that section."   1990 c. 8.

PART II

AMENDMENTS OF OTHER ACTS

National Parks and Access to the Countryside Act 1949 (c. 97)

12.—(1) Section 51 of the National Parks and Access to the Countryside Act 1949 (general provisions as to long-distance routes) is amended as follows.

(2) In subsection (2)(a), for the words from "any public path" to the end there is substituted "any highway along which the route passes and which is a public path, a restricted byway or a way shown in a definitive map and statement as a restricted byway or byway open to all traffic;".

(3) In subsection (5), for the words from "existing public paths" to "route passes" there is substituted "existing highways falling within paragraph (a) of that subsection".

(4) After that subsection there is inserted—

"(6) In this section—

"definitive map and statement" has the same meaning as in Part III of the Wildlife and Countryside Act 1981; and

"restricted byway" has the same meaning as in Part II of the Countryside and Rights of Way Act 2000."

13.—(1) Section 57 of that Act (penalty for displaying on footpaths notices deterring public use) is amended as follows.

(2) In subsection (1), for "road used as a public path" there is substituted "restricted byway".

(3) In subsection (3), for "or road used as a public path" there is substituted "restricted byway or byway open to all traffic".

(4) After that subsection there is inserted—

"(4) In this section—

"byway open to all traffic" has the same meaning as in Part III of the Wildlife and Countryside Act 1981;

"restricted byway" has the same meaning as in Part II of the Countryside and Rights of Way Act 2000."

Countryside Act 1968 (c. 41)

14. In section 41(11) of the Countryside Act 1968 (power to make byelaws and related provision about wardens)—

(a) for "road used as a public path" there is substituted "restricted byway", and

(b) after "27(6) of the Act of 1949" there is inserted "and section 48(4) of the Countryside and Rights of Way Act 2000".

Highways Act 1980 (c. 66)

15. In section 116 of the 1980 Act (power of magistrates' court to authorise stopping up or diversion of highway) in subsection (4), for "or bridleway" there is substituted ", bridleway or restricted byway".

16. In section 329 of the 1980 Act (interpretation)—

(a) in subsection (1) after the definition of "reconstruction" there is inserted—

""restricted byway" has the same meaning as in Part II of the Countryside and Rights of Way Act 2000;",

(b) in subsection (2) for "either "bridleway" or "footpath"" there is substituted ""bridleway", "footpath" or "restricted byway"".

Criminal Justice and Public Order Act 1994 (c. 33)

17. In section 61 of the Criminal Justice and Public Order Act 1994 (power to remove trespassers on land), in paragraph (b)(i) of the definition of "land" in subsection (9) for the words from "it falls" to "public path)" there is substituted "it is a footpath, bridleway or byway open to all traffic within the meaning of Part III of the Wildlife and Countryside Act 1981, is a restricted byway within the meaning of Part II of the Countryside and Rights of Way Act 2000".

Section 57.

SCHEDULE 6

Amendments relating to creation, stopping up and diversion of highways

Part I

Amendments of Highways Act 1980

1. In section 26 of the 1980 Act (compulsory powers for creation of footpaths and bridleways) after subsection (3) there is inserted—

"(3A) The considerations to which—

    (a) the Secretary of State is to have regard in determining whether or not to confirm or make a public path creation order, and

    (b) a local authority are to have regard in determining whether or not to confirm such an order as an unopposed order,

include any material provision of a rights of way improvement plan prepared by any local highway authority whose area includes land over which the proposed footpath or bridleway would be created."

2. For section 29 of the 1980 Act there is substituted—

"Duty to have regard to agriculture, forestry and nature conservation.

29.—(1) In the exercise of their functions under this Part of this Act relating to the making of public path creation agreements and public path creation orders it shall be the duty of councils to have due regard to—

    (a) the needs of agriculture and forestry, and

    (b) the desirability of conserving flora, fauna and geological and physiographical features.

(2) In this section, "agriculture" includes the breeding or keeping of horses."

3. In section 31 of the 1980 Act (dedication of way as highway presumed after public use for 20 years), in subsection (6), in each of paragraphs (i) and (ii) for "six" there is substituted "ten".

4. After section 31 of the 1980 Act there is inserted—

"Register of maps, statements and declarations.

31A.—(1) The appropriate council shall keep, in such manner as may be prescribed, a register containing such information as may be prescribed with respect to maps and statements deposited and declarations lodged with that council under section 31(6) above.

(2) Regulations may make provision for the register to be kept in two or more parts, each part containing such information as may be prescribed with respect to such maps, statements and declarations.

(3) Regulations may make provision as to circumstances in which an entry relating to a map, statement or declaration, or anything relating to it, is to be removed from the register or from any part of it.

(4) Every register kept under this section shall be available for inspection free of charge at all reasonable hours.

(5) In this section—

    "appropriate council" has the same meaning as in section 31(6) above;

"prescribed" means prescribed by regulations;

"regulations" means regulations made by the Secretary of State."

5. In section 36 of the 1980 Act (highways maintainable at public expense) in subsection (2), after paragraph (e) there is inserted—

"(f) a highway, being a footpath, a bridleway, a restricted byway or a way over which the public have a right of way for vehicular and all other kinds of traffic, created in consequence of a special diversion order or an SSSI diversion order."

6. In section 118 of the 1980 Act (stopping up of footpaths and bridleways) after subsection (6) there is inserted—

"(6A) The considerations to which—

(a) the Secretary of State is to have regard in determining whether or not to confirm a public path extinguishment order, and

(b) a council are to have regard in determining whether or not to confirm such an order as an unopposed order,

include any material provision of a rights of way improvement plan prepared by any local highway authority whose area includes land over which the order would extinguish a public right of way."

7. After section 118 of the 1980 Act there is inserted—

"Application for a public path extinguishment order.

118ZA.—(1) The owner, lessee or occupier of any land used for agriculture, forestry or the breeding or keeping of horses may apply to a council for the area in which the land is situated for the making of a public path extinguishment order in relation to any footpath or bridleway which crosses the land.

(2) An application under this section shall be in such form as may be prescribed and shall be accompanied by a map, on such scale as may be prescribed, showing the land over which it is proposed that the public right of way should be extinguished, and by such other information as may be prescribed.

(3) Regulations may provide—

(a) that a prescribed charge is payable on the making of an application under this section, and

(b) that further prescribed charges are payable by the applicant if the council make a public path extinguishment order on the application.

(4) An application under this section is not to be taken to be received by the council until the requirements of regulations under section 121A below have been satisfied in relation to it.

(5) A council which receives an application under this section shall determine the application as soon as reasonably practicable.

(6) Before determining to make a public path extinguishment order on an application under this section, the council may require the applicant to enter into an agreement with them to defray, or to make such contribution as may be specified in the agreement towards, any compensation which may become payable under section 28 above as applied by section 121(2) below.

(7) Where—

    (a) an application under this section has been made to a council, and

    (b) the council have not determined the application within four months of receiving it,

the Secretary of State may, at the request of the applicant and after consulting the council, by direction require the council to determine the application before the end of such period as may be specified in the direction.

(8) As soon as practicable after determining an application under this section, the council shall—

    (a) give to the applicant notice in writing of their decision and the reasons for it, and

    (b) give a copy of the notice to such other persons as may be prescribed.

(9) The council to whom an application under this section has been made may make a public path extinguishment order on the application only if the land over which the public right of way is to be extinguished by the order is that shown for the purposes of subsection (2) above on the map accompanying the application.

(10) Any reference in this Act to the map accompanying an application under this section includes a reference to any revised map submitted by the applicant in prescribed circumstances in substitution for that map.

(11) This section has effect subject to the provisions of sections 121A and 121C below.

(12) In this section—

    "prescribed" means prescribed by regulations;

    "regulations" means regulations made by the Secretary of State."

8. After section 118A of the 1980 Act there is inserted—

"Stopping up of certain highways for purposes of crime prevention, etc.

118B.—(1) This section applies where it appears to a council—

    (a) that, as respects any relevant highway for which they are the highway authority and which is in an area designated by the Secretary of State by order for the purposes of this section, the conditions in subsection (3) below are satisfied and it is expedient, for the purpose of preventing or reducing crime which would otherwise disrupt the life of the community, that the highway should be stopped up, or

    (b) that, as respects any relevant highway for which they are the highway authority and which crosses land occupied for the purposes of a school, it is expedient, for the purpose of protecting the pupils or staff from—

        (i) violence or the threat of violence,

        (ii) harassment,

        (iii) alarm or distress arising from unlawful activity, or

(iv) any other risk to their health or safety arising from such activity,

that the highway should be stopped up.

(2) In subsection (1) above "relevant highway" means—

(a) any footpath, bridleway or restricted byway,

(b) any highway which is shown in a definitive map and statement as a footpath, a bridleway, or a restricted byway, but over which the public have a right of way for vehicular and all other kinds of traffic, or

(c) any highway which is shown in a definitive map and statement as a byway open to all traffic,

but does not include a highway that is a trunk road or a special road.

(3) The conditions referred to in subsection (1)(a) above are—

(a) that premises adjoining or adjacent to the highway are affected by high levels of crime, and

(b) that the existence of the highway is facilitating the persistent commission of criminal offences.

(4) Where this section applies, the council may by order made by them and submitted to and confirmed by the Secretary of State, or confirmed as an unopposed order, extinguish the public right of way over the highway.

(5) An order under subsection (4) above is in this Act referred to as a "special extinguishment order".

(6) Before making a special extinguishment order, the council shall consult the police authority for the area in which the highway lies.

(7) The Secretary of State shall not confirm a special extinguishment order made by virtue of subsection (1)(a) above, and a council shall not confirm such an order as an unopposed order, unless he or, as the case may be, they are satisfied that the conditions in subsection (3) above are satisfied, that the stopping up of the highway is expedient as mentioned in subsection (1)(a) above and that it is expedient to confirm the order having regard to all the circumstances, and in particular to—

(a) whether and, if so, to what extent the order is consistent with any strategy for the reduction of crime and disorder prepared under section 6 of the Crime and Disorder Act 1998,

(b) the availability of a reasonably convenient alternative route or, if no reasonably convenient alternative route is available, whether it would be reasonably practicable to divert the highway under section 119B below rather than stopping it up, and

(c) the effect which the extinguishment of the right of way would have as respects land served by the highway, account being taken of the provisions as to compensation contained in section 28 above as applied by section 121(2) below.

(8) The Secretary of State shall not confirm a special extinguishment order made by virtue of subsection (1)(b) above, and a council shall not confirm such an order as an

1998 c. 37.

unopposed order unless he or, as the case may be, they are satisfied that the stopping up of the highway is expedient as mentioned in subsection (1)(b) above and that it is expedient to confirm the order having regard to all the circumstances, and in particular to—

(a) any other measures that have been or could be taken for improving or maintaining the security of the school,

(b) whether it is likely that the coming into operation of the order will result in a substantial improvement in that security,

(c) the availability of a reasonably convenient alternative route or, if no reasonably convenient alternative route is available, whether it would be reasonably practicable to divert the highway under section 119B below rather than stopping it up, and

(d) the effect which the extinguishment of the right of way would have as respects land served by the highway, account being taken of the provisions as to compensation contained in section 28 above as applied by section 121(2) below.

(9) A special extinguishment order shall be in such form as may be prescribed by regulations made by the Secretary of State and shall contain a map, on such scale as may be prescribed, defining the land over which the public right of way is thereby extinguished.

(10) Schedule 6 to this Act has effect as to the making, confirmation, validity and date of operation of special extinguishment orders.

Application by proprietor of school for special extinguishment order.

118C.—(1) The proprietor of a school may apply to a council for the making by virtue of section 118B(1)(b) above of a special extinguishment order in relation to any highway for which the council are the highway authority and which—

(a) crosses land occupied for the purposes of the school, and

(b) is a relevant highway as defined by section 118B(2) above.

(2) Subsections (2) to (11) of section 118ZA above shall apply to applications under this section as they apply to applications under that section, with the substitution for references to a public path extinguishment order of references to a special extinguishment order; and regulations made under that section by virtue of this subsection may make different provision for the purposes of this section and for the purposes of that section.".

9.—(1) Section 119 of the 1980 Act (diversion of footpaths and bridleways) is amended as follows.

(2) In subsection (1)(b), for "so specified" there is substituted "specified in the order or determined".

(3) For subsection (3), there is substituted—

"(3) Where it appears to the council that work requires to be done to bring the new site of the footpath or bridleway into a fit condition for use by the public, the council shall—

(a) specify a date under subsection (1)(a) above, and

(b) provide that so much of the order as extinguishes (in accordance with subsection (1)(b) above) a public right of way is not to come into force until the local highway authority for the new path or way certify that the work has been carried out.".

(4) In subsection (5)—

(a) after "diversion order" there is inserted "on an application under section 119ZA below or", and

(b) for "him" there is substituted "the person who made the application or representations".

(5) After subsection (6) there is inserted—

"(6A) The considerations to which—

(a) the Secretary of State is to have regard in determining whether or not to confirm a public path diversion order, and

(b) a council are to have regard in determining whether or not to confirm such an order as an unopposed order,

include any material provision of a rights of way improvement plan prepared by any local highway authority whose area includes land over which the order would create or extinguish a public right of way."

10. After section 119 of the 1980 Act there is inserted—

"Application for a public path diversion order.

119ZA.—(1) Subject to subsection (2) below, the owner, lessee or occupier of any land used for agriculture, forestry or the breeding or keeping of horses may apply to a council for the area in which the land is situated for the making of a public path diversion order in relation to any footpath or bridleway which crosses the land, on the ground that in his interests it is expedient that the order should be made.

(2) No application may be made under this section for an order which would create a new footpath or bridleway communicating with—

(a) a classified road,

(b) a special road,

(c) a GLA road, or

(d) any highway not falling within paragraph (a) or (b) above for which the Minister is the highway authority,

unless the application is made with the consent of the highway authority for the way falling within paragraph (a), (b), (c) or (d) above.

(3) No application under this section may propose the creation of a new right of way over land covered by works used by any statutory undertakers for the purposes of their undertaking or the curtilage of such land, unless the application is made with the consent of the statutory undertakers; and in this subsection "statutory undertaker" and "statutory undertaking" have the same meaning as in Schedule 6 to this Act.

(4) An application under this section shall be in such form as may be prescribed and shall be accompanied by a map, on such scale as may be prescribed—

(a) showing the existing site of so much of the line of the path or way as it is proposed to divert and the new site to which it is proposed to be diverted,

(b) indicating whether it is proposed to create a new right of way over the whole of the new site or whether some of it is already comprised in a footpath or bridleway, and

(c) where some part of the new site is already so comprised, defining that part,

and by such other information as may be prescribed.

(5) Regulations may provide—

(a) that a prescribed charge is payable on the making of an application under this section, and

(b) that further prescribed charges are payable by the applicant if the council make a public path diversion order on the application.

(6) An application under this section is not to be taken to be received by the council until the requirements of regulations under section 121A below have been satisfied in relation to it.

(7) A council which receives an application under this section shall determine the application as soon as reasonably practicable.

(8) Where—

(a) an application under this section has been made to a council, and

(b) the council have not determined the application within four months of receiving it,

the Secretary of State may, at the request of the applicant and after consulting the council, by direction require the council to determine the application before the end of such period as may be specified in the direction.

(9) As soon as practicable after determining an application under this section, the council shall—

(a) give to the applicant notice in writing of their decision and the reasons for it, and

(b) give a copy of the notice to such other persons as may be prescribed.

(10) The council to whom an application under this section has been made may make a public path diversion order on the application only if—

(a) the land over which the public right of way is to be extinguished by the order, and

(b) the new site to which the path or way is to be diverted,

are those shown for the purposes of subsection (4) above on the map accompanying the application.

(11) Any reference in this Act to the map accompanying an application under this section includes a reference to any revised map submitted by the applicant in prescribed circumstances in substitution for that map.

(12) This section has effect subject to the provisions of sections 121A and 121C below.

(13) In this section—

"prescribed" means prescribed by regulations;

"regulations" means regulations made by the Secretary of State."

11.—(1) Section 119A (diversion of footpaths and bridleways crossing railways) is amended as follows.

(2) In subsection (2)(b), for "so specified" there is substituted "specified in the order or determined under subsection (7) below".

(3) For subsection (7) there is substituted—

"(7) Where it appears to the council that work requires to be done to bring the new site of the footpath or bridleway into a fit condition for use by the public, the council shall—

(a) specify a date under subsection (2)(a) above, and

(b) provide that so much of the order as extinguishes (in accordance with subsection (2)(b) above) a public right of way is not to come into force until the local highway authority for the new path or way certify that the work has been carried out.".

12. After section 119A of the 1980 Act there is inserted—

"Diversion of certain highways for purposes of crime prevention, etc.

119B.—(1) This section applies where it appears to a council—

(a) that, as respects any relevant highway for which they are the highway authority and which is in an area designated by the Secretary of State by order under section 118B(1)(a) above, the conditions in subsection (3) below are satisfied and it is expedient, for the purpose of preventing or reducing crime which would otherwise disrupt the life of the community, that the line of the highway, or part of that line should be diverted (whether on to land of the same or another owner, lessee or occupier), or

(b) that, as respects any relevant highway for which they are the highway authority and which crosses land occupied for the purposes of a school, it is expedient, for the purpose of protecting the pupils or staff from—

(i) violence or the threat of violence,

(ii) harassment,

(iii) alarm or distress arising from unlawful activity, or

(iv) any other risk to their health or safety arising from such activity,

that the line of the highway, or part of that line, should be diverted (whether on to land of the same or another owner, lessee or occupier).

(2) In subsection (1) above "relevant highway" means—

(a) any footpath, bridleway or restricted byway,

(b) any highway which is shown in a definitive map and statement as a footpath, a bridleway, or a restricted byway, but over which the public have a right of way for vehicular and all other kinds of traffic, or

(c) any highway which is shown in a definitive map and statement as a byway open to all traffic,

but does not include a highway that is a trunk road or a special road.

(3) The conditions referred to in subsection (1)(a) above are—

   (a) that premises adjoining or adjacent to the highway are affected by high levels of crime, and

   (b) that the existence of the highway is facilitating the persistent commission of criminal offences.

(4) Where this section applies, the council may by order made by them and submitted to and confirmed by the Secretary of State, or confirmed as an unopposed order—

   (a) create, as from such date as may be specified in the order, any such—

        (i) new footpath, bridleway or restricted byway, or

        (ii) in a case falling within subsection (2)(b) or (c) above, new highway over which the public have a right of way for vehicular and all other kinds of traffic,

      as appears to the council requisite for effecting the diversion, and

   (b) extinguish, as from such date as may be specified in the order or determined in accordance with the provisions of subsection (8) below, the public right of way over so much of the highway as appears to the council to be requisite for the purpose mentioned in paragraph (a) or (b) of subsection (1) above.

(5) An order under subsection (4) above is in this Act referred to as a "special diversion order".

(6) Before making a special diversion order, the council shall consult the police authority for the area in which the highway is situated.

(7) A special diversion order shall not alter a point of termination of the highway—

   (a) if that point is not on a highway, or

   (b) (where it is on a highway) otherwise than to another point which is on the same highway, or a highway connected with it.

(8) Where it appears to the council that work requires to be done to bring the new site of the highway into a fit condition for use by the public, the council shall—

   (a) specify a date under subsection (4)(a) above, and

   (b) provide that so much of the order as extinguishes (in accordance with subsection (4)(b) above) a public right of way is not to come into force until the local highway authority for the new highway certify that the work has been carried out.

(9) A right of way created by a special diversion order may be either unconditional or (whether or not the right of way extinguished by the order was subject to limitations or conditions of any description) subject to such limitations or conditions as may be specified in the order.

(10) The Secretary of State shall not confirm a special diversion order made by virtue of subsection (1)(a) above, and a council shall not confirm such an order as an unopposed order unless he or, as the case may be, they are satisfied that the

conditions in subsection (3) above are satisfied, that the diversion of the highway is expedient as mentioned in subsection (1)(a) above and that it is expedient to confirm the order having regard to all the circumstances, and in particular to—

(a) whether and, if so, to what extent the order is consistent with any strategy for the reduction of crime and disorder prepared under section 6 of the Crime and Disorder Act 1998,

(b) the effect which the coming into operation of the order would have as respects land served by the existing public right of way, and

(c) the effect which any new public right of way created by the order would have as respects the land over which the right is so created and any land held with it,

so, however, that for the purposes of paragraphs (b) and (c) above the Secretary of State or, as the case may be, the council shall take into account the provisions as to compensation contained in section 28 above as applied by section 121(2) below.

(11) The Secretary of State shall not confirm a special diversion order made by virtue of subsection (1)(b) above, and a council shall not confirm such an order as an unopposed order unless he or, as the case may be, they are satisfied that the diversion of the highway is expedient as mentioned in subsection (1)(b) above and that it is expedient to confirm the order having regard to all the circumstances, and in particular to—

(a) any other measures that have been or could be taken for improving or maintaining the security of the school,

(b) whether it is likely that the coming into operation of the order will result in a substantial improvement in that security,

(c) the effect which the coming into operation of the order would have as respects land served by the existing public right of way, and

(d) the effect which any new public right of way created by the order would have as respects the land over which the right is so created and any land held with it,

so, however, that for the purposes of paragraphs (c) and (d) above the Secretary of State or, as the case may be, the council shall take into account the provisions as to compensation contained in section 28 above as applied by section 121(2) below.

(12) A special diversion order shall be in such form as may be prescribed by regulations made by the Secretary of State and shall contain a map, on such scale as may be so prescribed—

(a) showing the existing site of so much of the line of the highway as is to be diverted by the order and the new site to which it is to be diverted,

(b) indicating whether a new right of way is created by the order over the whole of the new site or whether some part of it is already comprised in a highway, and

(c) where some part of the new site is already so comprised, defining that part.

(13) Schedule 6 to this Act has effect as to the making, confirmation, validity and date of operation of special diversion orders.

(14) Section 27 above (making up of new footpaths and bridleways) applies to a highway created by a special diversion order with the substitution—

 (a) for references to a footpath or bridleway of references to a footpath, a bridleway, a restricted byway or a highway over which the public have a right of way for vehicular and all other kinds of traffic,

 (b) for references to a public path creation order of references to a special diversion order, and

 (c) for references to section 26(2) above of references to section 120(3) below.

(15) Neither section 27 nor section 36 above is to be regarded as obliging a highway authority to provide on any highway created by a special diversion order a metalled carriage-way.

Application by proprietor of school for special diversion order.

119C.—(1) The proprietor of a school may apply to a council for the making by virtue of section 119B(1)(b) above of a special diversion order in relation to any highway for which the council are the highway authority and which—

 (a) crosses land occupied for the purposes of the school, and

 (b) is a relevant highway as defined by section 119B(2) above.

(2) No application may be made under this section for an order which would create a new highway communicating with—

 (a) a classified road,

 (b) a special road,

 (c) a GLA road, or

 (d) any highway not falling within paragraph (a) or (b) above for which the Minister is the highway authority,

unless the application is made with the consent of the highway authority for the way falling within paragraph (a), (b), (c) or (d) above.

(3) Before determining to make a special diversion order on an application under this section, the council may require the applicant to enter into an agreement with them to defray, or to make such contribution as may be specified in the agreement towards—

 (a) any compensation which may become payable under section 28 above as applied by section 121(2) below, or

 (b) to the extent that the council are the highway authority for the highway in question, any expenses which they may incur in bringing the new site of the highway into fit condition for use by the public, or

 (c) to the extent that the council are not the highway authority, any expenses which may become recoverable from them by the highway authority under the provisions of section 27(2) above as applied by section 119B(14) above.

(4) Subsections (3) to (12) of section 119ZA above shall apply to applications under this section as they apply to applications under that section, with the substitution—

(a) for references to a public path diversion order of references to a special diversion order, and

(b) for references to a footpath or bridleway of references to a highway,

and regulations made under that section by virtue of this subsection may make different provision for the purposes of this section and for the purposes of that section.

Diversion of certain highways for protection of sites of special scientific interest.

119D.—(1) Subsection (3) below applies where, on an application made in accordance with this section by the appropriate conservation body, it appears to a council, as respects any relevant highway for which they are the highway authority and which is in, forms part of, or is adjacent to or contiguous with, a site of special scientific interest—

(a) that public use of the highway is causing, or that continued public use of the highway is likely to cause, significant damage to the flora, fauna or geological or physiographical features by reason of which the site of special scientific interest is of special interest, and

(b) that it is expedient that the line of the highway, or part of that line should be diverted (whether on to land of the same or another owner, lessee or occupier) for the purpose of preventing such damage.

(2) In subsection (1) "relevant highway" means—

(a) a footpath, bridleway or restricted byway,

(b) a highway which is shown in a definitive map and statement as a footpath, a bridleway or a restricted byway but over which the public have a right of way for vehicular and all other kinds of traffic, or

(c) any highway which is shown in a definitive map and statement as a byway open to all traffic,

but does not include any highway that is a trunk road or special road.

(3) Where this subsection applies, the council may, by order made by them and submitted to and confirmed by the Secretary of State, or confirmed as an unopposed order,—

(a) create, as from such date as may be specified in the order, any such—

(i) new footpath, bridleway or restricted byway, or

(ii) in a case falling within subsection (2)(b) or (c) above, new highway over which the public have a right of way for vehicular and all other kinds of traffic,

as appears to the council requisite for effecting the diversion, and

(b) extinguish, as from such date as may be specified in the order or determined in accordance with the provisions of subsection (6) below, the public right of way over so much of the way as appears to the council to be requisite for the purpose mentioned in subsection (1)(b) above.

(4) An order under this section is referred to in this Act as an "SSSI diversion order".

(5) An SSSI diversion order shall not alter a point of termination of the highway—

(a) if that point is not on a highway, or

(b) (where it is on a highway) otherwise than to another point which is on the same highway, or a highway connected with it.

(6) Where it appears to the council that work requires to be done to bring the new site of the highway into a fit condition for use by the public, the council shall—

(a) specify a date under subsection (3)(a) above, and

(b) provide that so much of the order as extinguishes (in accordance with subsection (3)(b) above) a public right of way is not to come into force until the local highway authority for the new highway certify that the work has been carried out.

(7) A right of way created by an SSSI diversion order may be either unconditional or (whether or not the right of way extinguished by the order was subject to limitations or conditions of any description) subject to such limitations or conditions as may be specified in the order.

(8) Before determining to make an SSSI diversion order, the council may require the appropriate conservation body to enter into an agreement with them to defray, or to make such contribution as may be specified in the agreement towards,—

(a) any compensation which may become payable under section 28 above as applied by section 121(2) below,

(b) to the extent that the council are the highway authority for the highway, any expenses which they may incur in bringing the new site of the highway into fit condition for use for the public, or

(c) to the extent that the council are not the highway authority, any expenses which may become recoverable from them by the highway authority under the provisions of section 27(2) above as applied by section 119E(6) below.

(9) The Secretary of State shall not confirm an SSSI diversion order, and a council shall not confirm such an order as an unopposed order, unless he, or as the case may be, they are satisfied that the conditions in subsection (1)(a) and (b) are satisfied, and that it is expedient to confirm the order having regard to the effect which—

(a) the diversion would have on public enjoyment of the right of way as a whole;

(b) the coming into operation of the order would have as respects other land served by the existing public right of way; and

(c) any new public right of way created by the order would have as respects the land over which the right is so created and any land held with it,

so, however, that for the purposes of paragraphs (b) and (c) above the Secretary of State or, as the case may be, the council shall take into account the provisions as to compensation referred to in subsection (8)(a) above.

(10) Schedule 6 to this Act has effect as to the making, confirmation, validity and date of operation of SSSI diversion orders.

(11) This section has effect subject to section 119E below.

(12) In this section—

"the appropriate conservation body" means—

(a) as respects England, English Nature, and

(b) as respects Wales, the Countryside Council for Wales;

1981 c. 69.

"site of special scientific interest" has the same meaning as in the Wildlife and Countryside Act 1981.

Provisions supplementary to section 119D.

119E.—(1) An application under section 119D above shall be in such form as may be prescribed and shall be accompanied by—

(a) a map, on such scale as may be prescribed,—

(i) showing the existing site of so much of the line of the highway as would be diverted if the order were made and the new site to which it would be diverted,

(ii) indicating whether a new right of way would be created by the order over the whole of the new site or whether some of it is already comprised in a highway, and

(iii) where some part of the new site is already so comprised, defining that part,

(b) by an assessment in the prescribed form of the effects of public use of the right of way on the site of special scientific interest, and

(c) by such other information as may be prescribed.

(2) At least fourteen days before making an application under section 119D above, the appropriate conservation body shall give a notice in the prescribed form of their intention to do so—

(a) to any owner, lessee or occupier of land over which the proposed order would create or extinguish a public right of way;

(b) to such other persons as may be prescribed; and

(c) in the case of English Nature, to the Countryside Agency.

(3) A council, in determining whether it is expedient to make or confirm an SSSI diversion order, and the Secretary of State, in determining whether to confirm such an order, shall, in particular, have regard to the following questions—

(a) whether the council would be able to prevent damage of the kind referred to in section 119D(1) above by making a traffic regulation order, and

(b) if so, whether the making of a traffic regulation order would cause less inconvenience to the public than that which would be caused by the diversion of the highway.

(4) The Secretary of State, in determining whether it is expedient to make an SSSI diversion order under section 120(3) below in a case where by virtue of section 22(4) of the Road

Traffic Regulation Act 1984 he has power to make a traffic regulation order shall, in particular, have regard to the following questions—

(a) whether he would be able to prevent damage of the kind referred to in section 119D(1) above by making a traffic regulation order, and

(b) if so, whether the making of a traffic regulation order would cause less inconvenience to the public than that which would be caused by the diversion of the highway.

(5) An SSSI diversion order shall be in such form as may be prescribed and shall contain a map, on such scale as may be prescribed,—

(a) showing the existing site of so much of the line of the highway as is to be diverted by the order and the new site to which it is to be diverted,

(b) indicating whether a new right of way is created by the order over the whole of the new site or whether some part of it is already comprised in a highway, and

(c) where some part of the new site is already so comprised, defining that part.

(6) Section 27 above (making up of new footpaths and bridleways) applies to a highway created by an SSSI diversion order with the substitution—

(a) for references to a footpath or bridleway of references to a footpath, a bridleway, a restricted byway or a highway over which the public have a right of way for vehicular and all other kinds of traffic,

(b) for references to a public path creation order, of references to an SSSI diversion order, and

(c) for references to section 26(2) above, of references to section 120(3) below.

(7) Neither section 27 nor section 36 above is to be regarded as obliging a highway authority to provide on any highway created by an SSSI diversion order a metalled carriage-way.

(8) In this section—

"the appropriate conservation body" has the same meaning as in section 119D above;

"prescribed" means prescribed by regulations made by the Secretary of State;

"site of special scientific interest" has the same meaning as in the Wildlife and Countryside Act 1981;

"traffic regulation order" means an order under section 1 or 6 of the Road Traffic Regulation Act 1984."

13.—(1) Section 120 of the 1980 Act (exercise of powers of making public path extinguishment and diversion orders) is amended as follows.

(2) In subsection (1), for "to 119A" there is substituted ", 118A, 119 and 119A".

(3) After that subsection there is inserted—

"(1A) Where a council are the highway authority for only part of a highway, the powers conferred on the council by sections 118B, 119B and 119D above are exercisable with respect to the whole of the highway, but subject to subsection (2) and only with the consent of every other council which is a highway authority for any other part with respect to which the powers are exercised."

(4) In subsection (2)—

  (a) for "to 119A" there is substituted "to 119D", and

  (b) for "footpath or bridleway", wherever occurring, there is substituted "highway".

(5) In subsection (3)—

  (a) after "or diverted" there is inserted "or where it appears to the Secretary of State as respects a relevant highway as defined by section 118B(2), 119B(2) or 119D(2) that it is expedient as mentioned in section 118B(1)(a) or (b), 119B(1)(a) or (b) or 119D(1)(b) that the highway should be stopped up or diverted",

  (b) in paragraph (a), for "a rail crossing diversion order or a public path diversion order" there is substituted "a special extinguishment order, a public path diversion order, a rail crossing diversion order, a special diversion order or an SSSI diversion order",

  (c) in paragraph (b), for "to 119A" there is substituted "to 119D",

  (d) for "(subject to subsection (3A) below)" there is substituted "(subject to the following provisions of this section)", and

  (e) at the end there is inserted "and, in the case of an SSSI diversion order, with the appropriate conservation body".

(6) After subsection (3) there is inserted—

"(3ZA) Where an appeal to the Secretary of State is brought under section 121D(1) below, paragraph (a) of subsection (3) above does not apply, and the power conferred on him by that subsection may be exercised without consultation with the appropriate authority."

(7) After subsection (3A) there is inserted—

"(3B) Unless an appeal to the Secretary of State is brought under section 121D(1) below, the power conferred on the Secretary of State by subsection (3) above to make a special extinguishment order or a special diversion order is exercisable only after consultation with the police authority in whose area the highway lies.

(3C) The power conferred on the Secretary of State by subsection (3) above to make an SSSI diversion order may be exercised even though the appropriate conservation body has not made an application under section 119D above to the council who are the highway authority for the highway.

(3D) Where—

  (a) the appropriate conservation body has made an application under section 119D above to a council in respect of a highway for which the council are the highway authority, and

  (b) the council have neither confirmed the order nor submitted it to the Secretary of State for confirmation within 6 months of receiving the application,

the power conferred on the Secretary of State by subsection (3) above to make an SSSI diversion order may be exercised without consultation with the council."

(8) In subsection (4)—

  (a) for "or a rail crossing diversion order" there is substituted ", a rail crossing diversion order, a special diversion order or an SSSI diversion order", and

  (b) for "path or way" there is substituted "highway".

(9) For subsection (5) there is substituted—

"(5) The Secretary of State may, before determining—

(a) under subsection (3) above, to make a public path diversion order,

(b) under subsection (3) above, to make a public path extinguishment order, special extinguishment order, public path diversion order or special diversion order on an appeal under section 121D(1)(a) below,

(c) to confirm a public path extinguishment order, special extinguishment order, public path diversion order or special diversion order in respect of which an appeal under section 121D(1)(b) or (c) below has been brought, or

(d) under subsection (3) above, to make a rail crossing diversion order on the representations of the operator of the railway concerned,

require the appropriate person to enter into such agreement as he may specify with such council has he may specify for that person to defray, or to make such contribution as may be specified in the agreement towards, any such compensation or expenses as are specified in paragraphs (a), (b) and (c) of section 119(5), or as the case may be, section 118ZA(6), 119A(8) or 119C(3) above.

(6) In subsection (5) above "the appropriate person" means—

(a) in a case falling within paragraph (a) of that subsection—

(i) where an appeal under section 121D(1)(a) below has been brought, the appellant, or

(ii) in any other case, the person on whose representations the Secretary of State is acting,

(b) in a case falling within paragraph (b) or (c) of that subsection, the appellant, and

(c) in a case falling within paragraph (d) of that subsection, the operator of the railway concerned."

(10) After subsection (6) there is inserted—

"(7) Where under subsection (3) above the Secretary of State decides to make an SSSI diversion order he may require the appropriate conservation body to enter into an agreement with such council as he may specify for the body to defray, or to make such contribution as may be specified in the agreement towards, any such compensation or expenses as are specified in paragraphs (a), (b) and (c) of section 119D(8) above.

(8) In this section "the appropriate conservation body" has the same meaning as in section 119D above."

14.—(1) Section 121 of the 1980 Act (supplementary provisions as to public path extinguishment and diversion orders) is amended as follows.

(2) In subsection (1)—

(a) after "rail crossing extinguishment order," there is inserted "a special extinguishment order",

(b) for "or a rail crossing diversion order", wherever occurring, there is substituted ", a rail crossing diversion order, a special diversion order or an SSSI diversion order", and

(c) for "path or way", wherever occurring, there is substituted "highway".

(3) In subsection (2)—

(a) after "rail crossing extinguishment orders," there is inserted "special extinguishment orders",

(b) for "and rail crossing diversion orders" there is substituted ", rail crossing diversion orders, special diversion orders and SSSI diversion orders", and

(c) for the words from "but" onwards there is substituted—

"but as if—

(a) the references in it to section 26(2) above were references to section 120(3) above, and

(b) in relation to special extinguishment orders, special diversion orders and SSSI diversion orders, the reference in section 28(4) to a footpath or bridleway included a reference to a restricted byway or a highway over which the public have a right of way for vehicular and all other kinds of traffic.".

(4) In subsection (3)—

(a) for "(protection for agriculture and forestry)" there is substituted "(duty to have regard to agriculture, forestry and nature conservation)",

(b) after "rail crossing extinguishment orders," there is inserted "special extinguishment orders", and

(c) for "and rail crossing diversion orders" there is substituted ", rail crossing diversion orders, special diversion orders and SSSI diversion orders".

(5) In subsection (4)—

(a) after "rail crossing extinguishment order," there is inserted "a special extinguishment order", and

(b) for "or a rail crossing diversion order" there is substituted ", a rail crossing diversion order, a special diversion order or an SSSI diversion order".

(6) After subsection (5) there is inserted—

"(5A) Before making a determination under subsection (5) above the appropriate Minister may, if he thinks fit, give any person an opportunity to be heard on the question, and he must either give such an opportunity or cause a local inquiry to be held if a request to be heard with respect to the question to be determined is made—

(a) by the statutory undertakers,

(b) in the case of an order made on an application under section 118ZA, 118C, 119ZA or 119C above, by the person who made the application, and

(c) in the case of an order to be made on an appeal under section 121D(1)(a) below, by the appellant.

(5B) The appropriate Minister may appoint any person to exercise on his behalf, with or without payment, the function of determining a question falling to be determined under subsection (5) above.

(5C) Schedule 12ZA to this Act shall have effect with respect to appointments under subsection (5B) above; and subsection (5A) above has effect subject to the provisions of that Schedule.

(5D) Subsections (2) to (5) of section 250 of the Local Government Act 1972 (giving of evidence at, and defraying of costs of, inquiries) shall apply in relation to hearings or local inquiries which the appropriate Minister causes to be held under subsection (5A) above as they apply (by virtue of section 302(1) of this Act) to local inquiries which the Secretary of State causes to be held under this Act.

1990 c. 8.

(5E) Section 322A of the Town and Country Planning Act 1990 (orders as to costs where no hearing or inquiry takes place) applies in relation to a hearing or inquiry under subsection (5A) above as it applies in relation to a hearing or local inquiry for the purposes referred to in that section, but as if references to the Secretary of State were references to the appropriate Minister."

(7) In subsection (6), for "subsection (5)" there is substituted "subsections (5) to (5E)".

15. After section 121 of the 1980 Act there is inserted—

"Regulations with respect to applications for orders.

121A.—(1) The Secretary of State may by regulations make provision as respects applications under section 118ZA, 118C, 119ZA or 119C above—

    (a) requiring the applicant to issue a certificate as to the interests in, or rights in or over, the land to which the application relates and the purpose for which the land is used,

    (b) requiring the applicant to give notice of the application to such persons as may be prescribed,

    (c) requiring the applicant to certify that any requirement of regulations under this section has been complied with or to provide evidence that any such requirement has been complied with,

    (d) as to the publicising of any application,

    (e) as to the form, content and service of such notices and certificates, and

    (f) as to the remission or refunding in prescribed circumstances of the whole or part of any prescribed charge.

(2) If any person—

    (a) issues a certificate which purports to comply with any requirement imposed by virtue of subsection (1) above and contains a statement which he knows to be false or misleading in a material particular; or

    (b) recklessly issues a certificate which purports to comply with any such requirement and contains a statement which is false or misleading in a material particular,

he shall be guilty of an offence.

(3) A person guilty of an offence under this section shall be liable on summary conviction to a fine not exceeding level 5 on the standard scale.

(4) Notwithstanding section 127 of the Magistrates' Courts Act 1980 (limitation of time for taking proceedings) summary proceedings for an offence under this section may be instituted at any time within three years after the commission of the offence.

Register of applications.

121B.—(1) Every council shall keep, in such manner as may be prescribed, a register containing such information as may be prescribed with respect to applications under section 118ZA, 118C, 119ZA or 119C above.

(2) The register shall contain such information as may be prescribed with respect to the manner in which such applications have been dealt with.

(3) Regulations may make provision for the register to be kept in two or more parts, each part containing such information relating to applications under section 118ZA, 118C, 119ZA or 119C above as may be prescribed.

(4) Regulations may make provision—

  (a) for a specified part of the register to contain copies of applications and of the maps submitted with them, and

  (b) for the entry relating to any application, and everything relating to it, to be removed from any part of the register when the application (including any appeal to the Secretary of State) has been finally disposed of (without prejudice to the inclusion of any different entry relating to it in another part of the register).

(5) Every register kept under this section shall be available for inspection by the public free of charge at all reasonable hours.

(6) In this section—

"prescribed" means prescribed by regulations;

"regulations" means regulations made by the Secretary of State.

Cases where council may decline to determine applications.

121C.—(1) A council may decline to determine an application under section 118ZA, 118C, 119ZA or 119C above if, within the period of three years ending with the date on which the application is received, the Secretary of State—

  (a) has refused to make an order on an appeal under section 121D(1)(a) below in respect of a similar application, or

  (b) has refused to confirm an order which is similar to the order requested.

(2) Before declining under subsection (1) above to determine an application under section 118C or 119C above, the council shall consider whether since the previous decision of the Secretary of State was made the risks referred to in subsection (1)(b)(i) to (iv) of section 118B or of section 119B have substantially increased.

(3) A council may decline to determine an application under section 118ZA, 118C, 119ZA or 119C above if—

  (a) in respect of an application previously made to them under that section which is similar to the current application or relates to any of the land to which the current application relates, the council have not yet determined whether to make a public path extinguishment order, special extinguishment order, public path diversion order or special diversion order, or

  (b) the council have made a similar order or an order which relates to any of the land to which the current application relates but no final decision as to the confirmation of the order has been taken.

(4) For the purposes of this section an application or order is similar to a later application or order only if they are, in the opinion of the council determining the later application, the

same or substantially the same, but an application or order may be the same or substantially the same as a later application or order even though it is made to or by a different council.

Right of appeal to Secretary of State in respect of applications for orders.

121D.—(1) Subject to the provisions of this section, where, in relation to an application made under section 118ZA, 118C, 119ZA or 119C above, the council to which the application was made—

    (a) refuse to make an order on the application,

    (b) refuse to confirm as an unopposed order an order made on the application, or

    (c) refuse to submit to the Secretary of State an order which is made on the application and against which any representation or objection has been duly made and not withdrawn,

the applicant may, by giving notice to the Secretary of State, appeal to the Secretary of State.

(2) Subsection (1)(a) above does not confer any right to appeal to the Secretary of State where—

    (a) the council have no power to make the order requested without the consent of another person and that consent has not been given, or

    (b) the reason, or one of the reasons, for the refusal to make the order is that the applicant has refused to enter into an agreement required by the council—

        (i) in the case of a public path extinguishment order, under subsection (6) of section 118ZA above,

        (ii) in the case of a special extinguishment order, under that subsection as applied by section 118C(2) above,

        (iii) in the case of a public path diversion order, under section 119(5) above,

        (iv) in the case of a special diversion order, under section 119C(3) above.

(3) Paragraph (b) of subsection (1) above does not confer any right to appeal to the Secretary of State in a case where the council has no power to confirm the order without the consent of another person and that consent has not been given; and paragraph (c) of that subsection does not confer any right to appeal to the Secretary of State in a case where, if the order had been unopposed, the council would have had no power to confirm it without the consent of another person and that consent has not been given.

Determination of appeals.

121E.—(1) Where an appeal to the Secretary of State is brought under section 121D(1)(a) above, the Secretary of State shall—

    (a) prepare a draft of a public path extinguishment order, special extinguishment order, public path diversion order or special diversion order under section 120(3) above giving effect to the application and containing such other provisions as, after consultation with such persons as he thinks fit, the Secretary of State may determine,

    (b) give notice of the draft order in accordance with paragraph 1(2) of Schedule 6 to this Act, and

(c) subject to subsection (6) below and to paragraph 2 of that Schedule, determine whether to make the order (with or without modifications) under section 120(3) above.

(2) Where an appeal to the Secretary of State is brought under section 121D(1)(b) or (c) above, the order made on the application shall be treated as having been submitted to him for confirmation (with or without modifications).

(3) Where an appeal to the Secretary of State is brought under section 121D(1) above, the Secretary of State may not make or confirm a public path diversion order or special diversion order if it appears to him that—

(a) work is necessary to bring the new highway created by the order into a fit condition for use by the public,

(b) if the order were made, the work could not be carried out by the highway authority without—

(i) the consent of another person, or

(ii) any authorisation (however described) which is required by or under any enactment, and

(c) the consent or authorisation has not been obtained.

(4) Where an appeal to the Secretary of State is brought under section 121D(1) above, the Secretary of State may not—

(a) make a public path diversion order or special diversion order so as to create a public right of way over land covered by works used for the purposes of a statutory undertaking or the curtilage of such land, or

(b) modify such an order so as to create such a public right of way,

unless the statutory undertaker has consented to the making or modification of the order.

(5) In subsection (4) above "statutory undertaker" and "statutory undertaking" have the same meaning as in Schedule 6 to this Act.

(6) Subsection (1)(c) above does not apply where any consent required by section 121(4) above has not been obtained.

(7) The Secretary of State may by regulations make further provision with respect to appeals under section 121D(1) above.

(8) Regulations under subsection (7) above may, in particular, make provision—

(a) as to the manner in which, and time within which, notice of an appeal is to be given,

(b) as to the provision of information to the Secretary of State by the council to which the application to which the appeal relates was made,

(c) for the payment by the applicant of any expenses incurred by the Secretary of State—

(i) in preparing a draft order,

(ii) in giving any notice required by subsection (1)(b) above or Schedule 6 to this Act,

(d) requiring the production by the council to whom the application was made of any certificates required by regulations under section 121A(1)(a) above,

(e) requiring the applicant to give notice of the appeal to such persons as may be prescribed,

(f) requiring the applicant to certify that any requirement of regulations under this section has been complied with or to provide evidence that any such requirement has been complied with,

(g) as to the publicising of any appeal,

(h) as to the form, content and service of such notices and certificates,

(i) modifying the provisions of Schedule 6 to this Act in their application to the procedure on appeals under section 121D(1) above, and

(j) as to the remission or refunding in prescribed circumstances of any prescribed charge.

(9) The Secretary of State may by regulations provide that section 28 above, as applied by section 121(2) above, is to have effect in cases where a public path extinguishment order, special extinguishment order, public path diversion order or special diversion order is made under section 120(3) above on an appeal under section 121D(1)(a) above, as if the reference to such one of the authorities referred to as may be nominated by the Secretary of State were a reference to such one of those authorities as may be specified in, or determined in accordance with, the regulations.

(10) Subsections (2) to (4) of section 121A above shall apply in relation to any certificate purporting to comply with a requirement imposed by virtue of this section as they apply to a certificate purporting to comply with a requirement imposed by virtue of subsection (1) of that section.

(11) For the purposes of this section—

(a) a draft public path extinguishment order or special extinguishment order gives effect to an application under section 118ZA or 118C above only if the land over which the public right of way is to be extinguished by the order is that shown for the purposes of subsection (2) of section 118ZA above (or that subsection as applied by section 118C(2) above) on the map accompanying the application, and

(b) a draft public path diversion order or draft special diversion order gives effect to an application made to a council under section 119ZA or 119C above only if—

(i) the land over which the public right of way is to be extinguished by the order, and

(ii) the new site to which the highway is to be diverted,

are those shown for the purposes of subsection (4) of section 119ZA above (or that subsection as applied by section 119C(4) above) on the map accompanying the application.

(12) In this section "prescribed" means prescribed by regulations made by the Secretary of State."

16. After section 135 of the 1980 Act there is inserted—

"Temporary
diversion for
dangerous works.

135A.—(1) Where works of a prescribed description are likely to cause danger to users of a footpath or bridleway which passes over any land, the occupier of the land may, subject to the provisions of this section, temporarily divert—

(a) so much of the footpath or bridleway as passes over that land, and

(b) so far as is requisite for effecting that diversion, so much of the footpath or bridleway as passes over other land occupied by him.

(2) A person may not under this section divert any part of a footpath or bridleway if—

(a) the period or periods for which that part has been diverted under this section, and

(b) the period or periods for which any other part of the same footpath or bridleway passing over land occupied by him has been diverted under this section,

amount in aggregate to more than fourteen days in any one calendar year.

(3) Where a person diverts a footpath or bridleway under this section—

(a) he shall do so in a manner which is reasonably convenient for the exercise of the public right of way, and

(b) where the diversion is by means of a temporary footpath or bridleway, he shall so indicate the line of the temporary footpath or bridleway on the ground to not less than the minimum width that it is apparent to members of the public wishing to use it.

(4) This section does not authorise a person—

(a) to divert a footpath or bridleway on to land not occupied by him without the consent of the occupier of that land and of any other person whose consent is needed to obtain access to it,

(b) to divert a footpath onto a highway other than a footpath or bridleway, or

(c) to divert a bridleway onto a highway other than a bridleway.

(5) The person by whom a footpath or bridleway is diverted under this section shall—

(a) at least fourteen days before the commencement of the diversion, give notice of the diversion in accordance with subsection (6) below,

(b) at least seven days before the commencement of the diversion, publish notice of the diversion in a local newspaper circulating in the area in which the footpath or bridleway is situated, and

(c) display such notices as may be prescribed at such places, in such manner and at such times before or during the diversion as may be prescribed.

(6) Notice under subsection (5)(a) above shall be given—

(a) to the highway authority for the footpath or bridleway,

    (b) if the footpath or bridleway is on or contiguous with access land in England, to the Countryside Agency, and

    (c) if the footpath or bridleway is on or contiguous with access land in Wales, to the Countryside Council for Wales.

(7) A notice under subsection (5)(a), (b) or (c) above shall be in such form and contain such information as may be prescribed.

(8) If a person—

    (a) in a notice which purports to comply with the requirements of subsection (5)(a) or (b) above, makes a statement which he knows to be false in a material particular,

    (b) by a notice displayed on or near a footpath or bridleway, falsely purports to be authorised under this section to divert the footpath or bridleway, or

    (c) in diverting a footpath or bridleway under this section, fails to comply with subsection (3) above,

he shall be guilty of an offence and liable to a fine not exceeding level 3 on the standard scale.

(9) In this section—

"access land" has the same meaning as in Part I of the Countryside and Rights of Way Act 2000;

"minimum width" in relation to a temporary footpath or bridleway, means the minimum width, within the meaning of Schedule 12A to this Act, of the footpath or bridleway diverted;

"prescribed" means prescribed by regulations made by the Secretary of State.

Temporary diversion for dangerous works: supplementary.

135B.—(1) The person by whom a footpath or bridleway is diverted under section 135A above shall, before the diversion ceases to be authorised by that section, make good any damage to the footpath or bridleway resulting from the works mentioned in subsection (1) of that section, and remove from the footpath or bridleway any obstruction resulting from those works.

(2) Any person who fails to comply with the duty imposed on him by subsection (1) above is guilty of an offence and liable to a fine not exceeding level 3 on the standard scale.

(3) The highway authority may make good any damage, or remove any obstruction, in respect of which any person has failed to comply with that duty and recover from that person the amount of any expenses reasonably incurred by them in or in connection with doing so.

(4) Paragraph 3(1) of Schedule 12A to this Act does not apply in relation to any disturbance of the surface of a footpath or bridleway which subsection (1) above requires any person to make good; but paragraphs 7 and 8 of that Schedule apply for the purposes of subsection (3) above as if—

    (a) references to the authority were references to the highway authority,

> > (b) references to the work were references to work carried out under subsection (3) above in relation to a footpath or bridleway, and
> >
> > (c) references to the relevant land were references to the land over which the footpath or bridleway passes.
>
> (5) The diversion of a footpath or bridleway under section 135A above does not—
>
> > (a) affect the liability of any person for anything done in relation to the path or way otherwise than for the purposes of or in consequence of the works mentioned in subsection (1) of that section, or
> >
> > (b) authorise any interference with the apparatus or works of any statutory undertakers.
>
> (6) Without prejudice to section 130 (protection of public rights of way) above, it is the duty of the highway authority to enforce the provisions of section 135A and this section."

17. In section 293 of the 1980 Act (powers of entry for purposes connected with certain orders relating to footpaths and bridleways), in subsection (1)—

> (a) after "rail crossing extinguishment order," there is inserted "a special extinguishment order", and
>
> (b) for "or a rail crossing diversion order" there is substituted ", a rail crossing diversion order, a special diversion order or an SSSI diversion order".

18. In section 325 of the 1980 Act (regulations, schemes and orders)—

> (a) in subsection (1)(d), for "118, 119," there is substituted "118, 118A, 118B(4), 119, 119A, 119B(4), 119D", and
>
> (b) in subsection (2)(b), after "17" there is inserted "or 118B(1)(a)".

19. In section 326 of the 1980 Act (revocation and variation of schemes and orders) in subsection (5), for "a public path diversion order" there is substituted "a rail crossing extinguishment order, a special extinguishment order, a public path diversion order, a rail crossing diversion order, a special diversion order or an SSSI diversion order".

20. In section 329(1) of the 1980 Act (interpretation)—

> (a) after the definition of "cycle track" there is inserted—
>
> > ""definitive map and statement" has the same meaning as in Part III of the Wildlife and Countryside Act 1981;",
>
> (b) after the definition of "proposed highway" there is inserted—
>
> > ""proprietor", in relation to a school, has the same meaning as in the Education Act 1996;",
>
> (c) after the definition of "road-ferry" there is inserted—
>
> > ""school" has the same meaning as in the Education Act 1996;",
>
> (d) after the definition of "service area" there is inserted—
>
> > ""special diversion order" means an order under section 119B(4) above;",
>
> (e) after the definition of "special enactment" there is inserted—
>
> > ""special extinguishment order" means an order under section 118B(4) above;", and

1981 c. 69.

1996 c. 56.

(f) after the definition of "special road authority" there is inserted—

"'"SSSI diversion order" means an order under section 119D above;".

21. In section 334 of the 1980 Act (savings relating to telecommunications apparatus) in subsection (2), for "and a public path diversion order" there is substituted ", a special extinguishment order, a public path diversion order, a special diversion order and an SSSI diversion order".

22. In section 344 of the 1980 Act (application to Isles of Scilly) in subsection (2)(a) after "135," there is inserted "135A, 135B,".

23.—(1) Schedule 6 to the 1980 Act (provisions as to making, confirmation, validity and date of operation of certain orders relating to footpaths and bridleways), including that Schedule as applied by section 32(2) of the Acquisition of Land Act 1981, is amended as follows.

(2) In paragraph 1(1) and (2)—

    (a) after "rail crossing extinguishment order," there is inserted "a special extinguishment order", and

    (b) for "or a rail crossing diversion order" there is substituted ", a rail crossing diversion order, a special diversion order or an SSSI diversion order".

(3) In paragraph 1(3A)—

    (a) after "rail crossing extinguishment orders," there is inserted "special extinguishment orders", and

    (b) for "and rail crossing diversion orders" there is substituted ", rail crossing diversion orders, special diversion orders and SSSI diversion orders".

(4) In paragraph 1(3B)—

    (a) after "draft rail crossing extinguishment orders," there is inserted "draft special extinguishment orders", and

    (b) for "and draft rail crossing diversion orders" there is substituted ", draft rail crossing diversion orders, draft special diversion orders and draft SSSI diversion orders".

(5) In paragraph 2—

    (a) in sub-paragraph (1), at the beginning of paragraph (a) there is inserted "subject to sub-paragraph (2A)",

    (b) in sub-paragraphs (2) and (3), for "or a public path diversion order," there is substituted ", a public path diversion order, a special diversion order or an SSSI diversion order", and

    (c) after sub-paragraph (2) there is inserted—

"(2A) Before making or confirming an order on an appeal under section 121D(1) of this Act, the Secretary of State shall—

    (a) if requested by the authority who made an order to which the appeal relates to cause a local inquiry to be held, cause such an inquiry to be held, and

    (b) if a request to be heard with respect to the question to be determined is made by the appellant, either afford to the appellant an opportunity of being heard by a person appointed by the Secretary of State for the purpose or cause a local inquiry to be held,

whether or not he would be required to do so apart from this sub-paragraph."

(6) After paragraph 2 there is inserted—

"2ZA.—(1) Where a public path extinguishment order, a special extinguishment order, a public path diversion order or a special diversion order is made by an authority other than the Secretary of State on an application under section 118ZA, 118C, 119ZA or 119C of this Act, that authority shall, as soon as reasonably practicable after the expiry of the time for representations, determine—

(a) whether, in the case of an unopposed order, to confirm it under paragraph 2(1)(b) above, or

(b) whether to submit the order to the Secretary of State.

(2) The authority making a determination required by sub-paragraph (1) above shall, as soon as practicable after making it, give to the applicant notice in writing of their determination and the reasons for it and give a copy of the notice to such other persons as may be prescribed.

(3) Where—

(a) an authority other than the Secretary of State have made a public path extinguishment order, a special extinguishment order, a public path diversion order or a special diversion order on an application under section 118ZA, 118C, 119ZA or 119C of this Act, and

(b) at the end of the period of two months beginning with the expiry of the time for representations, that authority have not determined—

(i) whether, in the case of an unopposed order, to confirm it under paragraph 2(1)(b) above, or

(ii) whether to submit the order to the Secretary of State,

the Secretary of State may, at the request of the person on whose application the order was made, by direction require the authority to determine that question before the end of such period as may be specified in the direction.

(4) In this paragraph "the time for representations" means the time specified by the authority in accordance with paragraph 1(1)(c) above.

2ZB. Where, in relation to any public path extinguishment order, special extinguishment order, public path diversion order or special diversion order which was made by an authority other than the Secretary of State on an application under section 118ZA, 118C, 119ZA or 119C of this Act, no representations or objections are duly made or any representations or objections so made are withdrawn, that authority may not submit the order to the Secretary of State for confirmation with any modification of the map contained in the order."

(7) In paragraph 2A(1), for the words from the beginning to "shall" there is substituted—

"The following decisions—

(a) a decision of the Secretary of State under paragraph 2 above as respects an order made by an authority other than the Secretary of State including any related decision under section 120(5) of this Act, and

(b) a decision of the Secretary of State under section 121E(1)(c) of this Act, including any related decision under section 120(5) of this Act,

shall".

(8) After paragraph 2A there is inserted—

"2B.—(1) Subject to sub-paragraph (2), subsections (2) to (5) of section
250 of the Local Government Act 1972 (giving of evidence at, and   1972 c. 70.
defraying of costs of, inquiries) apply to a hearing which the Secretary of
State causes to be held under paragraph 2 above as they apply (by virtue
of section 302(1) of this Act) to a local inquiry which he causes to be held
under this Act.

(2) In its application to a hearing or local inquiry held under paragraph
2 above by a person appointed under paragraph 2A(1) above, subsection
(5) of section 250 of that Act shall have effect as if the reference to the
Minister causing the inquiry to be held were a reference to the person so
appointed or the Secretary of State.

(3) Section 322A of the Town and Country Planning Act 1990 (orders   1990 c. 8.
as to costs where no hearing or inquiry takes place) applies in relation to a
hearing or inquiry under paragraph 2 above as it applies in relation to a
hearing or local inquiry for the purposes referred to in that section.".

(9) In paragraph 3(2)—

    (a) for "or a rail crossing extinguishment order" there is substituted ", a rail
        crossing extinguishment order or a special extinguishment order", and

    (b) for "or a rail crossing diversion order" there is substituted ", a rail
        crossing diversion order, a special diversion order or an SSSI
        diversion order".

(10) At the end of paragraph 4(3) there is inserted "other than any person on
whom notice of the decision is required to be served under paragraph 2ZA(2)
above".

24. After Schedule 12 to the 1980 Act there is inserted—

"SCHEDULE 12ZA

DELEGATION OF FUNCTION OF MAKING DETERMINATION

Interpretation

1. In this Schedule—

    "appointed person" means a person appointed under section 121(5B)
    of this Act;

    "appropriate Minister" has the same meaning as in section 121(5) of
    this Act;

    "appointment", in the case of any appointed person, means
    appointment under section 121(5B) of this Act.

Appointments

2. An appointment under section 121(5B) of this Act must be in
writing and—

    (a) may relate to a particular question specified in the appointment or
        to questions of a description so specified,

    (b) may provide for any function to which it relates to be exercisable
        by the appointed person either unconditionally or subject to the
        fulfilment of such conditions as may be specified in the
        appointment, and

    (c) may, by notice in writing given to the appointed person, be
        revoked at any time by the appropriate Minister in respect of any
        question which has not been determined by the appointed person
        before that time.

SCH. 6

Powers of appointed person

3. Subject to the provisions of this Schedule, an appointed person shall, in relation to the determination of any question to which his appointment relates, have the same powers and duties as the appropriate Minister, other than—

   (a) any function of holding an inquiry or other hearing or of causing an inquiry or other hearing to be held; or

   (b) any function of appointing a person for the purpose—

      (i) of enabling persons to appear before and be heard by the person so appointed; or

      (ii) of referring any question or matter to that person.

Holding of inquiries and other hearings by appointed persons

4.—(1) If either of the following persons—

   (a) the statutory undertakers to which the question relates, and

   (b) in the case of an order to be made on an application under section 118ZA, 118C, 119ZA or 119C of this Act, the person who made the application,

express a wish to appear before and be heard by the appointed person, the appointed person shall give them an opportunity of appearing and being heard.

(2) Whether or not sub-paragraph (1) above applies, the appointed person—

   (a) may hold an inquiry or other hearing in connection with the determination of the question, and

   (b) shall, if the appropriate Minister so directs, hold an inquiry in connection with that determination.

(3) Where an appointed person holds an inquiry or other hearing by virtue of this Schedule, an assessor may be appointed by the appropriate Minister to sit with the appointed person at the inquiry or hearing and advise him on any matters arising, notwithstanding that the appointed person is to determine the question.

(4) Subject to paragraph 7 below, the costs of an inquiry or other hearing held under this Schedule shall be defrayed by the appropriate Minister.

Revocation of appointments and making of new appointments

5.—(1) Where under paragraph 2(c) above the appointment of the appointed person is revoked in respect of any question, the appropriate Minister shall, unless he proposes to determine the question himself, appoint another person under section 121(5B) of this Act to determine the question instead.

(2) Where such a new appointment is made, the consideration of the question, or any hearing in connection with it, shall be begun afresh.

(3) Nothing in sub-paragraph (2) above shall require any person to be given an opportunity of making fresh representations or modifying or withdrawing any representations already made.

Certain acts and omissions of appointed person to be treated as those of appropriate Minister

6.—(1) Anything done or omitted to be done by an appointed person in, or in connection with, the exercise or purported exercise of any function to which the appointment relates shall be treated for all purposes as done or omitted to be done by the appropriate Minister.

(2) Sub-paragraph (1) above does not apply—

(a) for the purposes of so much of any contract made between the appropriate Minister and the appointed person as relates to the exercise of the function, or

(b) for the purposes of any criminal proceedings brought in respect of anything done or omitted to be done as mentioned in that sub-paragraph.

Local inquiries and hearings: evidence and costs

7. Subsections (2) to (5) of section 250 of the Local Government Act 1972 (local inquiries: evidence and costs) shall apply to local inquiries or other hearings held under this Schedule by an appointed person as they apply to inquiries caused to be held under that section by a Minister, but as if—   1972 c. 70.

(a) in subsection (2) (evidence) the reference to the person appointed to hold the inquiry were a reference to the appointed person,

(b) in subsection (4) (recovery of costs of holding inquiry) references to the Minister causing the inquiry to be held were references to the appropriate Minister, and

(c) in subsection (5) (orders as to the costs of the parties) the reference to the Minister causing the inquiry to be held were a reference to the appointed person or the appropriate Minister."

Part II

Consequential amendments of other Acts

Norfolk and Suffolk Broads Act 1988 (c. 4)

25. In Schedule 3 to the Norfolk and Suffolk Broads Act 1988 (functions of Broads Authority), in paragraph 47 (footpaths and bridleways)—

(a) for "118 to 121" there is substituted "118 to 121E", and

(b) after "footpaths etc.)" there is inserted ", except sections 118B and 119B of that Act (stopping up and diversion for purposes of crime prevention, etc.),".

Environment Act 1995 (c. 25)

26. In Schedule 9 to the Environment Act 1995 (miscellaneous functions of National Park authorities), in paragraph 11 (footpaths and bridleways) for paragraph (c) there is substituted—

"(c) sections 118 to 121E (stopping up and diversion of public paths, etc.), except sections 118B and 119B (stopping up and diversion for purposes of crime prevention, etc.), and".

SCHEDULE 7   Section 67.

Driving of mechanically propelled vehicles elsewhere than on roads

National Parks and Access to the Countryside Act 1949 (c. 97)

1. In section 51(1) of the National Parks and Access to the Countryside Act 1949 (general provisions as to long-distance routes), for "not being a motor vehicle" there is substituted "not being a mechanically propelled vehicle".

SCH. 7

Countryside Act 1968 (c. 41)

2.—(1) Section 30 of the Countryside Act 1968 (riding of pedal cycles on bridleways) is amended as follows.

(2) In subsection (1), for "not being a motor vehicle" there is substituted "not being a mechanically propelled vehicle".

(3) For subsection (5) there is substituted—

"(5) In this section "mechanically propelled vehicle" does not include a vehicle falling within paragraph (c) of section 189(1) of the Road Traffic Act 1988."

Chronically Sick and Disabled Persons Act 1970 (c. 44)

3. In section 20 of the Chronically Sick and Disabled Persons Act 1970 (use of invalid carriages on highways), in subsection (1)(b) after "sections 1 to 4," there is inserted "21, 34,".

Road Traffic Act 1988 (c. 52)

4.—(1) Section 21 of the Road Traffic Act 1988 (prohibition of driving or parking on cycle tracks) is amended as follows.

(2) In subsection (1), for "motor" there is substituted "mechanically propelled".

(3) In subsection (3), after paragraph (a) there is inserted—

"(aa) in subsection (1) "mechanically propelled vehicle" does not include a vehicle falling within paragraph (a), (b) or (c) of section 189(1) of this Act,".

5. For section 34 of that Act there is substituted—

"Prohibition of driving mechanically propelled vehicles elsewhere than on roads.

34.—(1) Subject to the provisions of this section, if without lawful authority a person drives a mechanically propelled vehicle—

(a) on to or upon any common land, moorland or land of any other description, not being land forming part of a road, or

(b) on any road being a footpath, bridleway or restricted byway,

he is guilty of an offence.

(2) For the purposes of subsection (1)(b) above, a way shown in a definitive map and statement as a footpath, bridleway or restricted byway is, without prejudice to section 56(1) of the Wildlife and Countryside Act 1981, to be taken to be a way of the kind shown, unless (subject to section 34A of this Act) the contrary is proved.

1981 c. 69.

(3) It is not an offence under this section to drive a mechanically propelled vehicle on any land within fifteen yards of a road, being a road on which a motor vehicle may lawfully be driven, for the purpose only of parking the vehicle on that land.

(4) A person shall not be convicted of an offence under this section with respect to a vehicle if he proves to the satisfaction of the court that it was driven in contravention of this section for the purpose of saving life or extinguishing fire or meeting any other like emergency.

(5) It is hereby declared that nothing in this section prejudices the operation of—

(a) section 193 of the Law of Property Act 1925 (rights of the public over commons and waste lands), or   1925 c. 20.

(b) any byelaws applying to any land,

or affects the law of trespass to land or any right or remedy to which a person may by law be entitled in respect of any such trespass or in particular confers a right to park a vehicle on any land.

(6) Subsection (2) above and section 34A of this Act do not extend to Scotland.

(7) In this section—

"definitive map and statement" has the same meaning as in Part III of the Wildlife and Countryside Act 1981;   1981 c. 69.

"mechanically propelled vehicle" does not include a vehicle falling within paragraph (a), (b) or (c) of section 189(1) of this Act; and

"restricted byway" means a way over which the public have restricted byway rights within the meaning of Part II of the Countryside and Rights of Way Act 2000, with or without a right to drive animals of any description along the way, but no other rights of way.".

6. After that section there is inserted—

"Exceptions to presumption in section 34(2).

34A.—(1) Where a person is charged with an offence under section 34 of this Act in respect of the driving of any vehicle, it is open to that person to prove under subsection (2) of that section that a way shown in a definitive map and statement as a footpath, bridleway or restricted byway is not a way of the kind shown only—

(a) if he proves to the satisfaction of the court—

(i) that he was a person interested in any land and that the driving of the vehicle by him was reasonably necessary to obtain access to the land,

(ii) that the driving of the vehicle by him was reasonably necessary to obtain access to any land, and was for the purpose of obtaining access to the land as a lawful visitor, or

(iii) that the driving of the vehicle by him was reasonably necessary for the purposes of any business, trade or profession; or

(b) in such circumstances as may be prescribed by regulations made by the Secretary of State (and paragraph (a) above is without prejudice to this paragraph).

(2) In subsection (1) above—

"interest", in relation to land, includes any estate in land and any right over land, whether the right is exercisable by virtue of the ownership of an estate or interest in land or by virtue of a licence or agreement, and in particular includes rights of common and sporting rights, and the reference to a person interested in land shall be construed accordingly;

"lawful visitor", in relation to land, includes any person who enters the land for any purpose in the exercise of a right conferred by law."

7. In section 195 of that Act—

(a) in subsection (3), after "that section)" there is inserted "34A", and

(b) in subsection (4), after "14" there is inserted ", 34A".

Road Traffic Offenders Act 1988 (c. 53)

8. In Schedule 2 to the Road Traffic Offenders Act 1988 (prosecution and punishment of offences), in the second column of the entry in Part I relating to section 34 of the Road Traffic Act 1988, for "motor" there is substituted "mechanically propelled".

9. In Schedule 3 to that Act (fixed penalty offences), in the second column of the entry relating to section 34 of the Road Traffic Act 1988, for "motor" there is substituted "mechanically propelled".

Section 73(4).

SCHEDULE 8

AMENDMENTS CONSEQUENTIAL ON CHANGE OF NAME OF NATURE CONSERVANCY COUNCIL FOR ENGLAND

1. In each provision specified in relation to each of the Acts set out below, for "the Nature Conservancy Council for England" or, as the case may be, "Nature Conservancy Council for England" there is substituted "English Nature"—

1949 c.97.

(a) the National Parks and Access to the Countryside Act 1949: section 15A (meaning of "Nature Conservancy Council");

1966 c. 38.

(b) the Sea Fisheries Regulation Act 1966: in section 5A (byelaws under section 5 for marine environmental purposes), subsection (3)(a);

1968 c. 41.

(c) the Countryside Act 1968—

(i) in section 15 (areas of special scientific interest), subsection (6A), and

(ii) section 37 (protection for interests in countryside);

1970 c. 30.

(d) the Conservation of Seals Act 1970: in section 10 (power to grant licences to kill or take seals), subsection (5);

1980 c. 27.

(e) the Import of Live Fish (England and Wales) Act 1980: in section 1 (power to limit the import etc. of fish and fish eggs), subsection (2);

1980 c. 66.

(f) the Highways Act 1980: in section 105B (procedure relating to environmental impact assessments), in subsection (8), paragraph (b) of the definition of "the consultation bodies";

1981 c. 22.

(g) the Animal Health Act 1981: in section 21 (destruction of wild life on infection other than rabies), subsection (9);

1981 c. 69.

(h) the Wildlife and Countryside Act 1981—

(i) in section 27 (interpretation of Part I), subsection (3A),

(ii) in section 27A (construction of references to Nature Conservancy Council), paragraph (a), and

(iii) in section 52 (interpretation of Part II), subsection (1);

1984 c. 51.

(i) the Inheritance Tax Act 1984: Schedule 3 (bodies receiving gifts for national purposes etc.);

1986 c. 49.

(j) the Agriculture Act 1986: in section 18 (designation and management of environmentally sensitive areas), subsection (2)(a);

(k) the Channel Tunnel Act 1987—

(i) in Schedule 2, Part II (regulation of scheduled works), paragraph 5(3), and

(ii) in Schedule 3 (planning permission), paragraph 17(4)(a);

(l) the Norfolk and Suffolk Broads Act 1988—

(i) in section 1 (the Broads Authority), subsection (3)(b),

(ii) in section 4 (conservation of areas of natural beauty), subsections (3)(a) and (5)(a),

(iii) in section 5 (notification of certain operations within the Broads), subsection (4), and

(iv) in Schedule 3 (functions of Broads Authority), paragraph 33(1)(c);

(m) the Electricity Act 1989: in Schedule 9 (preservation of amenities and fisheries), paragraph 2(2)(a);

(n) the Environmental Protection Act 1990—

(i) in section 36 (grant of waste management licences), subsection (7), and

(ii) in section 128 (creation and constitution of the Nature Conservancy Council for England and the Countryside Council for Wales), subsections (1) and (2)(a);

(o) the Deer Act 1991: in section 8 (licences for exemptions from sections 2 to 4 of the Act), subsections (1) and (4);

(p) the Water Industry Act 1991—

(i) in section 4 (environmental duties with respect to sites of special interest), subsections (1) and (4),

(ii) in section 5 (codes of practice with respect to environmental and recreational duties), subsection (4)(b), and

(iii) in section 156 (restrictions on disposals of land), subsection (4)(c)(i);

(q) the Land Drainage Act 1991—

(i) in section 61C (duties with respect to sites of special scientific interest), subsections (1) and (4), and

(ii) in section 61E (codes of practice), subsection (4)(b);

(r) the Transport and Works Act 1992: in section 6 (applications for orders relating to railways, tramways, inland waterways, etc.), subsection (7)(e);

(s) the Protection of Badgers Act 1992: in section 10 (licences to do otherwise prohibited acts relating to badgers), subsection (4)(a);

(t) the Environment Act 1995—

(i) in section 8 (environmental duties with respect to sites of special interest), subsections (1) and (4),

(ii) in section 9 (codes of practice with respect to environmental and recreational duties), subsection (3)(b),

(iii) in section 66 (national park management plans), subsection (7)(a), and

(iv) in section 99 (consultation required before making or modifying certain subordinate legislation for England), subsection (2)(c);

(u) the Channel Tunnel Rail Link Act 1996—

(i) in Schedule 6 (planning conditions), paragraph 27(4), and

(ii) in Schedule 14 (overhead lines: consent), paragraph 7(4); and

SCH. 8
1999 c. 29.

(v) the Greater London Authority Act 1999: in section 352 (the Mayor's biodiversity action plan), subsection (3)(a).

2. In the following enactments, the entry for the Nature Conservancy Council for England is omitted, and in the appropriate place there is inserted "English Nature"—

1958 c. 51.

(a) the Public Records Act 1958: in Schedule 1 (definition of public records), Part II of the Table in paragraph 3;

1965 c. 74.

(b) the Superannuation Act 1965: in section 39 (meaning of "public office"), paragraph 7 of subsection (1); and

1967 c. 13.

(c) the Parliamentary Commissioner Act 1967: Schedule 2 (departments etc. subject to investigation).

1975 c. 24.

3. In Part III of Schedule 1 to the House of Commons Disqualification Act 1975 (which sets out offices the holders of which are disqualified from membership of the House of Commons), the entry for "Any member of the Nature Conservancy Council for England or the Countryside Council for Wales in receipt of remuneration" is omitted, and in the appropriate places there are inserted the following two entries—

"Any member of the Countryside Council for Wales in receipt of remuneration."

"Any member of English Nature in receipt of remuneration.".

Section 75(1).

SCHEDULE 9

SITES OF SPECIAL SCIENTIFIC INTEREST

1. For section 28 of the 1981 Act (areas of special scientific interest) there is substituted—

"Sites of special scientific interest.

28.—(1) Where the Nature Conservancy Council are of the opinion that any area of land is of special interest by reason of any of its flora, fauna, or geological or physiographical features, it shall be the duty of the Council to notify that fact—

(a) to the local planning authority in whose area the land is situated;

(b) to every owner and occupier of any of that land; and

(c) to the Secretary of State.

(2) The Council shall also publish a notification of that fact in at least one local newspaper circulating in the area in which the land is situated.

(3) A notification under subsection (1) shall specify the time (not being less than three months from the date of the giving of the notification) within which, and the manner in which, representations or objections with respect to it may be made; and the Council shall consider any representation or objection duly made.

(4) A notification under subsection (1)(b) shall also specify—

(a) the flora, fauna, or geological or physiographical features by reason of which the land is of special interest, and

(b) any operations appearing to the Council to be likely to damage that flora or fauna or those features,

and shall contain a statement of the Council's views about the management of the land (including any views the Council may have about the conservation and enhancement of that flora or fauna or those features).

(5) Where a notification under subsection (1) has been given, the Council may within the period of nine months beginning with the date on which the notification was served on the Secretary of State either—

(a) give notice to the persons mentioned in subsection (1) withdrawing the notification; or

(b) give notice to those persons confirming the notification (with or without modifications).

(6) A notification shall cease to have effect—

(a) on the giving of notice of its withdrawal under subsection (5)(a) to any of the persons mentioned in subsection (1); or

(b) if not withdrawn or confirmed by notice under subsection (5) within the period of nine months referred to there, at the end of that period.

(7) The Council's power under subsection (5)(b) to confirm a notification under subsection (1) with modifications shall not be exercised so as to add to the operations specified in the notification or extend the area to which it applies.

(8) As from the time when there is served on the owner or occupier of any land which has been notified under subsection (1)(b) a notice under subsection (5)(b) confirming the notification with modifications, the notification shall have effect in its modified form in relation to so much (if any) of that land as remains subject to it.

(9) A notification under subsection (1)(b) of land in England and Wales shall be a local land charge.

(10) For the purposes of this section and sections 28A to 28D, "local planning authority", in relation to land within the Broads, includes the Broads Authority.

Variation of notification under section 28.

28A.—(1) At any time after notice has been given under section 28(5)(b) confirming a notification (with or without modifications), the Nature Conservancy Council may by notice vary the matters specified or stated in the confirmed notification (whether by adding to them, changing them, or removing matter from them).

(2) The area of land cannot be varied under this section.

(3) The Council shall give notice setting out the variation to—

(a) the local planning authority in whose area the land is situated,

(b) every owner and occupier of any of the land who in the opinion of the Council may be affected by the variation, and

(c) the Secretary of State,

and after service of a notice under paragraph (b) the notification under section 28(1)(b) shall have effect in its varied form.

(4) Section 28(3) shall apply to such a notice as it applies to a notification under section 28(1).

(5) Where a notice under subsection (3) has been given, the Council may within the period of nine months beginning with the date the last of the owners and occupiers referred to in subsection (3)(b) was served with the notice either—

(a) give notice to the persons mentioned in subsection (3) withdrawing the notice; or

(b) give notice to them confirming the notice (with or without modifications).

(6) A notice under subsection (3) shall cease to have effect—

(a) on the giving of notice of its withdrawal under subsection (5)(a) to any of the persons mentioned in subsection (3); or

(b) if not withdrawn or confirmed by notice under subsection (5) within the period of nine months referred to in that subsection, at the end of that period.

(7) As from the time when there is served on the owner or occupier of any land a notice under subsection (5)(b) confirming a notice of variation with modifications, the notification under section 28(1)(b) shall have effect as so varied.

(8) A local land charge existing by virtue of section 28(9) shall be varied in accordance with a notice under subsection (3) or (5)(b).

Notification of additional land.

28B.—(1) Where the Nature Conservancy Council are of the opinion that if land adjacent to a site of special scientific interest ("the extra land") were combined with the site of special scientific interest ("the SSSI"), the combined area of land would be of special interest by reason of any of its flora, fauna, or geological or physiographical features, the Council may decide to notify that fact.

(2) If they do so decide, the persons whom they must notify are—

(a) the local planning authority in whose area the extra land is situated;

(b) every owner and occupier of any of that extra land; and

(c) the Secretary of State.

(3) No such notification may be given until after notice has been given under section 28(5)(b) confirming (with or without modifications) the notification under section 28(1) relating to the SSSI.

(4) Subsections (2) and (3) of section 28 shall apply for the purposes of this section as they apply for the purposes of that section.

(5) A notification under subsection (2)(b) shall also specify—

    (a) the area of land constituting the SSSI;

    (b) what (as at the date of the notification under subsection (2)(b)) is specified or contained in the notification under section 28(1)(b) relating to the SSSI by virtue of section 28(4); and

    (c) the reasons why the Council is of the opinion referred to in subsection (1).

(6) In addition, the notification under subsection (2)(b) shall include a statement—

    (a) saying whether or not anything among the matters specified in the notification by virtue of subsection (5)(c) is particularly relevant to the extra land; and

    (b) if any such thing is of particular relevance, specifying which.

(7) Subsections (5) to (7) of section 28 apply in relation to a notification under subsection (2) of this section as they apply in relation to a notification under subsection (1) of that section, as if references to "subsection (1)" in section 28(5) to (7) were references to subsection (2) of this section.

(8) As from the time when a notification under subsection (2)(b) is served on the owner or occupier of any land, the notification under section 28(1)(b) shall have effect as if it included the notification under subsection (2)(b).

(9) As from the time when there is served on the owner or occupier of any land which has been notified under subsection (2)(b) a notice under section 28(5)(b) (as applied by subsection (7) of this section) confirming the notification under subsection (2)(b) with modifications, the notification under section 28(1)(b) (as extended by virtue of subsection (8) of this section) shall have effect in its modified form.

(10) A local land charge existing by virtue of section 28(9) shall be varied in accordance with a notification under subsection (2) or under section 28(5)(b) as applied by subsection (7) of this section.

Enlargement of SSSI.

28C.—(1) Where the Nature Conservancy Council are of the opinion that any area of land which includes, but also extends beyond, a site of special scientific interest ("the SSSI") is of special interest by reason of any of its flora, fauna, or geological or physiographical features, the Council may decide to notify that fact.

(2) If they do so decide, the persons whom they must notify are—

    (a) the local planning authority in whose area the land (including the SSSI) is situated;

    (b) every owner and occupier of any of that land (including the SSSI); and

    (c) the Secretary of State.

(3) Subsections (2) to (8) of section 28 apply to a notification under subsection (2) of this section as they apply to a notification under subsection (1) of that section, as if references

to "subsection (1)" and "subsection (1)(b)" in section 28(2) to (8) were references to subsection (2) and subsection (2)(b) of this section respectively.

(4) No notification may be given under subsection (2) until after notice has been given under section 28(5)(b) (or section 28(5)(b) as applied by subsection (3)) confirming (with or without modifications) the notification under section 28(1) (or subsection (2)) relating to the SSSI.

(5) As from the time when a notification under subsection (2) is served on the owner or occupier of any land included in the SSSI, the notification in relation to that land which had effect immediately before the service of the notification under subsection (2) shall cease to have effect.

(6) A notification under subsection (2)(b) of land in England and Wales shall be a local land charge; and, to the extent that any such land was the subject of a local land charge by virtue of section 28(9), that local land charge shall be discharged.

(7) A notice under section 28E(1)(a) and a consent under section 28E(3)(a) given before a notification under subsection (2)(b) continue to have effect.

(8) The enlargement of a site of special scientific interest under this section does not affect anything done under section 28J to 28L.

(9) Any reference to—

(a) a notification under section 28(1) (or any of its paragraphs) shall be construed as including the corresponding notification under subsection (2);

(b) a notification under section 28(5)(b) shall be construed as including a notification under that provision as applied by subsection (3); and

(c) a local land charge existing by virtue of section 28(9) shall be treated as including one existing by virtue of subsection (6).

Denotification.

28D.—(1) Where the Nature Conservancy Council are of the opinion that all or part of a site of special scientific interest is no longer of special interest by reason of any of the matters mentioned in section 28(1), they may decide to notify that fact.

(2) If they do so decide, the persons whom they must notify are—

(a) the local planning authority in whose area the land which the Council no longer consider to be of special interest is situated;

(b) every owner and occupier of any of that land;

(c) the Secretary of State;

(d) the Environment Agency; and

(e) every relevant undertaker (within the meaning of section 4(1) of the Water Industry Act 1991) and every internal drainage board (within the meaning of section 61C(1) of the Land Drainage Act 1991) whose works, operations or activities may affect the land.

1991 c. 56.

1991 c. 59.

(3) The Council shall also publish a notification of that fact in at least one local newspaper circulating in the area in which the land referred to in subsection (2)(a) is situated.

(4) Section 28(3) shall apply to a notification under subsection (2) or (3) as it applies to a notification under section 28(1).

(5) Where a notification under subsection (2) has been given, the Council may within the period of nine months beginning with the date on which the notification was served on the Secretary of State either—

    (a) give notice to the persons mentioned in subsection (2) withdrawing the notification, or

    (b) give notice to those persons confirming the notification, or confirming it in relation to an area of land specified in the notice which is smaller than that specified in the notification under subsection (2),

but if they do neither the notification shall cease to have effect.

(6) A notification under subsection (2) shall have effect in relation to any land as from the time a notice under subsection (5)(b) is served on its owner or occupier, and from that time a notification under section 28(1)(b) in relation to that land shall cease to have effect.

(7) A local land charge existing by virtue of section 28(9) shall be discharged in relation to land which is the subject of a notice under subsection (5)(b).

Duties in relation to sites of special scientific interest.

28E.—(1) The owner or occupier of any land included in a site of special scientific interest shall not while the notification under section 28(1)(b) remains in force carry out, or cause or permit to be carried out, on that land any operation specified in the notification unless—

    (a) one of them has, after service of the notification, given the Nature Conservancy Council notice of a proposal to carry out the operation specifying its nature and the land on which it is proposed to carry it out; and

    (b) one of the conditions specified in subsection (3) is fulfilled.

(2) Subsection (1) does not apply to an owner or occupier being an authority to which section 28G applies acting in the exercise of its functions.

(3) The conditions are—

    (a) that the operation is carried out with the Council's written consent;

    (b) that the operation is carried out in accordance with the terms of an agreement under section 16 of the 1949 Act or section 15 of the 1968 Act;

    (c) that the operation is carried out in accordance with a management scheme under section 28J or a management notice under section 28K.

(4) A consent under subsection (3)(a) may be given—

    (a) subject to conditions, and

    (b) for a limited period,

as specified in the consent.

(5) If the Council do not consent, they shall give notice saying so to the person who gave the notice under subsection (1).

SCH. 9

(6) The Council may, by notice given to every owner and occupier of any of the land included in the site of special scientific interest, or the part of it to which the consent relates—

    (a) withdraw the consent; or

    (b) modify it (or further modify it) in any way.

(7) The following—

    (a) a consent under subsection (3)(a) granting consent subject to conditions or for a limited period, and

    (b) a notice under subsection (5) or (6),

must include a notice of the Council's reasons for imposing the conditions, for the limitation of the period, for refusing consent, or for withdrawing or modifying the consent, and also a notice of the matters set out in subsection (8).

(8) The matters referred to in subsection (7) are—

    (a) the rights of appeal under section 28F;

    (b) the effect of subsection (9); and

    (c) in the case of a notice under subsection (6), the effect of section 28M.

(9) A withdrawal or modification of a consent is not to take effect until—

    (a) the expiry of the period for appealing against it; or

    (b) if an appeal is brought, its withdrawal or final determination.

(10) The Council shall have power to enforce the provisions of this section.

Appeals in connection with consents.

28F.—(1) The following persons—

    (a) an owner or occupier who has been refused a consent under section 28E(3)(a),

    (b) an owner or occupier who has been granted such a consent but who is aggrieved by conditions attached to it, or by the fact that it is for a limited period, or by the length of that period,

    (c) an owner or occupier who is aggrieved by the modification of a consent;

    (d) an owner or occupier who is aggrieved by the withdrawal of a consent,

may by notice appeal to the Secretary of State against the relevant decision.

(2) If the Nature Conservancy Council neither give consent nor refuse it within the period of four months beginning with the date on which the notice referred to in section 28E(1)(a) was sent, the person who gave that notice may for the purposes of subsection (1) treat the Council as having refused consent (and his appeal is to be determined on that basis).

(3) Notice of an appeal must reach the Secretary of State—

    (a) except in a case falling within subsection (2), within the period of two months beginning with the date of the notice giving consent or the notice under section 28E(5) or (6), or

(b) in a case falling within subsection (2), within the period of two months beginning immediately after the expiry of the four-month period referred to there,

or, in either case, within such longer period as is agreed in writing between the Council and the appellant.

(4) Before determining an appeal, the Secretary of State may, if he thinks fit—

(a) cause the appeal to take, or continue in, the form of a hearing (which may be held wholly or partly in private if the appellant so requests and the person hearing the appeal agrees), or

(b) cause a local inquiry to be held,

and he must act as mentioned in paragraph (a) or (b) if either party to the appeal asks to be heard in connection with the appeal.

(5) On determining an appeal against a decision, the Secretary of State may—

(a) affirm the decision,

(b) where the decision was a refusal of consent, direct the Council to give consent,

(c) where the decision was as to the terms of a consent (whether the original or a modified one), quash all or any of those terms,

(d) where the decision was a withdrawal or modification of consent, quash the decision,

and where he exercises any of the powers in paragraphs (b), (c) or (d) he may give directions to the Council as to the terms on which they are to give consent.

(6) The Secretary of State may by regulations made by statutory instrument make provision about appeals under this section, and in particular about—

(a) notices of appeal and supporting documentation required, and

(b) how appeals are to be brought and considered,

and any such regulations may make different provision for different cases and circumstances.

(7) A statutory instrument containing regulations under subsection (6) shall be subject to annulment in pursuance of a resolution of either House of Parliament.

(8) The Secretary of State may appoint any person to exercise on his behalf, with or without payment, his function of determining an appeal under this section or any matter involved in such an appeal.

(9) Schedule 10A shall have effect with respect to appointments under subsection (8).

(10) Subsections (2) to (5) of section 250 of the Local Government Act 1972 (local inquiries: evidence and costs) apply in relation to hearings or local inquiries under this section as they apply in relation to local inquiries under that section, but as if the reference there—

1972 c. 70.

(a) to the person appointed to hold the inquiry were a reference to the Secretary of State or to the person appointed to conduct the hearing or hold the inquiry under this section; and

(b) to the Minister causing an inquiry to be held were to the Secretary of State.

1990 c. 8.

(11) Section 322A of the Town and Country Planning Act 1990 (orders as to costs where no hearing or inquiry takes place) applies in relation to a hearing or local inquiry under this section as it applies in relation to a hearing or local inquiry referred to in that section.

Statutory undertakers, etc.: general duty.

28G.—(1) An authority to which this section applies (referred to in this section and in sections 28H and 28I as "a section 28G authority") shall have the duty set out in subsection (2) in exercising its functions so far as their exercise is likely to affect the flora, fauna or geological or physiographical features by reason of which a site of special scientific interest is of special interest.

(2) The duty is to take reasonable steps, consistent with the proper exercise of the authority's functions, to further the conservation and enhancement of the flora, fauna or geological or physiographical features by reason of which the site is of special scientific interest.

(3) The following are section 28G authorities—

(a) a Minister of the Crown (within the meaning of the Ministers of the Crown Act 1975) or a Government department;

1975 c. 26.

(b) the National Assembly for Wales;

(c) a local authority;

(d) a person holding an office—

(i) under the Crown,

(ii) created or continued in existence by a public general Act of Parliament, or

(iii) the remuneration in respect of which is paid out of money provided by Parliament;

(e) a statutory undertaker (meaning the persons referred to in section 262(1), (3) and (6) of the Town and Country Planning Act 1990); and

(f) any other public body of any description.

Statutory undertakers, etc.: duty in relation to carrying out operations.

28H.—(1) A section 28G authority shall give notice to the Nature Conservancy Council before carrying out, in the exercise of its functions, operations likely to damage any of the flora, fauna or geological or physiographical features by reason of which a site of special scientific interest is of special interest.

(2) Subsection (1) applies even if the operations would not take place on land included in a site of special scientific interest.

(3) In response to the notice referred to in subsection (1), the Council may send a notice—

(a) saying that they do not assent to the proposed operations, or

(b) assenting to them (with or without conditions),

but if they do not send a notice under paragraph (b) within the period of 28 days beginning with the date of the notice under subsection (1) they shall be treated as having declined to assent.

(4) If the Council do not assent, or if the authority proposes to carry out the operations otherwise than in accordance with the terms of the Council's assent, the authority—

    (a) shall not carry out the operations unless the condition set out in subsection (5) is satisfied, and

    (b) shall comply with the requirements set out in subsection (6) when carrying them out.

(5) The condition is that the authority has, after the expiry of the period of 28 days beginning with the date of the notice under subsection (1), notified the Council of—

    (a) the date on which it proposes to start the operations (which must be after the expiry of the period of 28 days beginning with the date of the notification under this paragraph), and

    (b) how (if at all) it has taken account of any written advice it received from the Council, before the date of the notification under this paragraph, in response to the notice under subsection (1).

(6) The requirements are—

    (a) that the authority carry out the operations in such a way as to give rise to as little damage as is reasonably practicable in all the circumstances to the flora, fauna or geological or physiographical features by reason of which the site is of special interest (taking account, in particular, of any such advice as is referred to in subsection (5)(b)); and

    (b) that the authority restore the site to its former condition, so far as is reasonably practicable, if any such damage does occur.

Statutory undertakers, etc.: duty in relation to authorising operations.

28I.—(1) This section applies where the permission of a section 28G authority is needed before operations may be carried out.

(2) Before permitting the carrying out of operations likely to damage any of the flora, fauna or geological or physiographical features by reason of which a site of special scientific interest is of special interest, a section 28G authority shall give notice of the proposed operations to the Nature Conservancy Council.

(3) Subsection (2) applies even if the operations would not take place on land included in a site of special scientific interest.

(4) The authority shall wait until the expiry of the period of 28 days beginning with the date of the notice under subsection (2) before deciding whether to give its permission, unless the Nature Conservancy Council have notified the authority that it need not wait until then.

(5) The authority shall take any advice received from the Council into account—

    (a) in deciding whether or not to permit the proposed operations, and

    (b) if it does decide to do so, in deciding what (if any) conditions are to be attached to the permission.

(6) If the Council advise against permitting the operations, or advise that certain conditions should be attached, but the section 28G authority does not follow that advice, the authority—

    (a) shall give notice of the permission, and of its terms, to the Council, the notice to include a statement of how (if at all) the authority has taken account of the Council's advice, and

    (b) shall not grant a permission which would allow the operations to start before the end of the period of 21 days beginning with the date of that notice.

(7) In this section "permission", in relation to any operations, includes authorisation, consent, and any other type of permission (and "permit" and "permitting" are to be construed accordingly).

Management schemes.

28J.—(1) The Nature Conservancy Council may formulate a management scheme for all or part of a site of special scientific interest.

(2) A management scheme is a scheme for—

    (a) conserving the flora, fauna, or geological or physiographical features by reason of which the land (or the part of it to which the scheme relates) is of special interest; or

    (b) restoring them; or

    (c) both.

(3) The Council shall serve notice of a proposed management scheme on every owner and occupier of any of the land (or the part of it to which the scheme would relate); but it may be served on them only after they have been consulted about the proposed management scheme.

(4) The notice may be served with the notification referred to in section 28(1)(b) or afterwards.

(5) The owners and occupiers upon whom the notice must be served (referred to in this section as "the relevant owners and occupiers") are—

    (a) if it is served with the notification under section 28(1)(b), or later but before the notification referred to in section 28(5)(b), the owners and occupiers referred to in section 28(1)(b);

    (b) if it is served with the notification under section 28(5)(b) or later, the owners and occupiers of such of the land as remains subject to the notification.

(6) The notice of a proposed management scheme must include a copy of the proposed scheme.

(7) The notice must specify the time (not being less than three months from the date of the giving of the notice) within which, and the manner in which, representations or objections with respect to the proposed management scheme may be made; and the Council shall consider any representation or objection duly made.

(8) Where a notice under subsection (3) has been given, the Council may within the period of nine months beginning with the date on which the notice was served on the last of the relevant owners and occupiers either—

(a) give notice to the relevant owners and occupiers withdrawing the notice, or

(b) give notice to them confirming the management scheme (with or without modifications),

and if notice under paragraph (b) is given, the management scheme shall have effect from the time the notice is served on all of the relevant owners or occupiers.

(9) A notice under subsection (3) shall cease to have effect—

(a) on the giving of a notice of withdrawal under subsection (8)(a) to any of the relevant owners and occupiers; or

(b) if not withdrawn or confirmed by notice under subsection (8) within the period of nine months referred to there, at the end of that period.

(10) The Council's power under subsection (8)(b) to confirm a management scheme with modifications shall not be exercised so as to make complying with it more onerous.

(11) The Council may at any time cancel or propose the modification of a management scheme.

(12) In relation to—

(a) the cancellation of a management scheme, subsections (3) to (5) apply, and

(b) a proposal to modify a management scheme, subsections (3) to (10) apply,

as they apply in relation to a proposal for a management scheme.

(13) An agreement under section 16 of the 1949 Act or section 15 of the 1968 Act relating to a site of special scientific interest may provide for any matter for which a management scheme relating to that site provides (or could provide).

Management notices.

28K.—(1) Where it appears to the Nature Conservancy Council that—

(a) an owner or occupier of land is not giving effect to a provision of a management scheme, and

(b) as a result any flora, fauna or geological or physiographical features by reason of which the land is of special interest are being inadequately conserved or restored,

they may if they think fit serve a notice on him (a "management notice").

(2) They may not serve a management notice unless they are satisfied that they are unable to conclude, on reasonable terms, an agreement with the owner or occupier as to the management of the land in accordance with the management scheme.

(3) A management notice is a notice requiring the owner or occupier to—

(a) carry out such work on the land, and

(b) do such other things with respect to it,

as are specified in the notice, and to do so before the dates or within the periods so specified.

(4) The work and other things specified in the notice must appear to the Council to be measures which it is reasonable to require in order to ensure that the land is managed in accordance with the management scheme.

(5) The management notice must explain the effect of subsection (7) and (8) and of sections 28L and 28M(2) to (4).

(6) A copy of the management notice must be served on every other owner and occupier of the land.

(7) If any of the work or other things required by a management notice have not been done within the period or by the date specified in it, the Council may—

(a) enter the land, and any other land, and carry out the work, or do the other things; and

(b) recover from the owner or occupier upon whom the notice was served any expenses reasonably incurred by them in carrying out the work or doing the other things.

(8) If an appeal is brought against the management notice, and upon the final determination of the appeal the notice is affirmed (with or without modifications), subsection (7) applies as if the references there to the management notice were to the notice as affirmed.

Appeals against management notices.

28L.—(1) A person who is served with a management notice may appeal against its requirements to the Secretary of State; and a management notice does not take effect until—

(a) the expiry of the period for appealing against it; or

(b) if an appeal is brought, its withdrawal or final determination.

(2) An appeal may be on the ground that some other owner or occupier of the land should take all or any of the measures specified in the management notice, or should pay all or part of their cost.

(3) Where the grounds of appeal are, or include, that mentioned in subsection (2), the appellant must serve a copy of his notice of appeal on each other person referred to.

(4) Before determining an appeal, the Secretary of State may, if he thinks fit—

(a) cause the appeal to take, or continue in, the form of a hearing (which may be held wholly or partly in private if the appellant so requests and the person hearing the appeal agrees), or

(b) cause a local inquiry to be held,

and he must act as mentioned in paragraph (a) or (b) if either party to the appeal (or, in a case falling within subsection (2), any of the other persons mentioned there) asks to be heard in connection with the appeal.

(5) On determining the appeal, the Secretary of State may quash or affirm the management notice; and if he affirms it, he may do so either in its original form or with such modifications as he thinks fit.

(6) In particular, on determining an appeal whose grounds are, or include, those mentioned in subsection (2), the Secretary of State may—

(a) vary the management notice so as to impose its requirements (or some of them) upon any such other person as is referred to in the grounds; or

(b) determine that a payment is to be made by any such other person to the appellant.

(7) In exercising his powers under subsection (6), the Secretary of State must take into account, as between the appellant and any of the other people referred to in subsection (2)—

(a) their relative interests in the land (considering both the nature of the interests and the rights and obligations arising under or by virtue of them);

(b) their relative responsibility for the state of the land which gives rise to the requirements of the management notice; and

(c) the relative degree of benefit to be derived from carrying out the requirements of the management notice.

(8) The Secretary of State may by regulations made by statutory instrument make provision about appeals under this section, and in particular about—

(a) the period within which and the manner in which appeals are to be brought, and

(b) the manner in which they are to be considered,

and any such regulations may make different provision for different cases or circumstances.

(9) A statutory instrument containing regulations under subsection (8) shall be subject to annulment in pursuance of a resolution of either House of Parliament.

(10) The Secretary of State may appoint any person to exercise on his behalf, with or without payment, his function of determining an appeal under this section or any matter involved in such an appeal.

(11) Schedule 10A shall have effect with respect to appointments under subsection (10).

(12) Subsections (2) to (5) of section 250 of the Local Government Act 1972 (local inquiries: evidence and costs) apply in relation to hearings or local inquiries under this section as they apply in relation to local inquiries under that section, but as if the reference there—   1972 c. 70.

(a) to the person appointed to hold the inquiry were a reference to the Secretary of State or to the person appointed to conduct the hearing or hold the inquiry under this section; and

(b) to the Minister causing an inquiry to be held were to the Secretary of State.

(13) Section 322A of the Town and Country Planning Act 1990 (orders as to costs where no hearing or inquiry takes place) applies in relation to a hearing or local inquiry under this section as it applies in relation to a hearing or local inquiry referred to in that section.   1990 c. 8.

SCH. 9

Payments.

28M.—(1) Where the Council, under section 28E(6), modify or withdraw a consent, they shall make a payment to any owner or occupier of the land who suffers loss because of the modification or withdrawal.

(2) The Council may, if they think fit, make one or more payments to any owner or occupier of land in relation to which a management scheme under section 28J is in force.

(3) The amount of a payment under this section is to be determined by the Council in accordance with guidance given and published by the Ministers.

(4) Section 50(3) applies to the determination of the amount of payments under this section as it applies to the determination of the amount of payments under that section.

Compulsory purchase.

28N.—(1) The Nature Conservancy Council may in circumstances set out in subsection (2) acquire compulsorily all or any part of a site of special scientific interest.

(2) The circumstances are—

    (a) that the Council are satisfied that they are unable to conclude, on reasonable terms, an agreement with the owner or occupier as to the management of the land; or

    (b) that the Council have entered into such an agreement, but they are satisfied that it has been breached in such a way that the land is not being managed satisfactorily.

(3) A dispute about whether or not there has been a breach of the agreement for the purposes of subsection (2)(b) is to be determined by an arbitrator appointed by the Lord Chancellor.

(4) Where the Council have acquired land compulsorily under this section, they may—

    (a) manage it themselves; or

    (b) dispose of it, or of any interest in it, on terms designed to secure that the land is managed satisfactorily.

(5) Section 103 of the 1949 Act (general provisions as to acquisition of land) applies for the purposes of this section as it applies for the purposes of that Act.

Offences.

28P.—(1) A person who, without reasonable excuse, contravenes section 28E(1) is guilty of an offence and is liable on summary conviction to a fine not exceeding £20,000 or on conviction on indictment to a fine.

(2) A section 28G authority which, in the exercise of its functions, carries out an operation which damages any of the flora, fauna or geological or physiographical features by reason of which a site of special scientific interest is of special interest—

    (a) without first complying with section 28H(1), or

    (b) (if it has complied with section 28H(1)) without first complying with section 28H(4)(a),

is, unless there was a reasonable excuse for carrying out the operation without complying, guilty of an offence and is liable on summary conviction to a fine not exceeding £20,000 or on conviction on indictment to a fine.

(3) A section 28G authority acting in the exercise of its functions which, having complied with section 28H(1), fails

without reasonable excuse to comply with section 28H(4)(b) is guilty of an offence and is liable on summary conviction to a fine not exceeding £20,000 or on conviction on indictment to a fine.

(4) For the purposes of subsections (1), (2) and (3), it is a reasonable excuse in any event for a person to carry out an operation (or to fail to comply with a requirement to send a notice about it) if—

> (a) subject to subsection (5), the operation in question was authorised by a planning permission granted on an application under Part III of the Town and Country Planning Act 1990 or permitted by a section 28G authority which has acted in accordance with section 28I; or

1990 c. 8.

> (b) the operation in question was an emergency operation particulars of which (including details of the emergency) were notified to the Nature Conservancy Council as soon as practicable after the commencement of the operation.

(5) If an operation needs both a planning permission and the permission of a section 28G authority, subsection (4)(a) does not provide reasonable excuse unless both have been obtained.

(6) A person (other than a section 28G authority acting in the exercise of its functions) who without reasonable excuse—

> (a) intentionally or recklessly destroys or damages any of the flora, fauna, or geological or physiographical features by reason of which land is of special interest, or intentionally or recklessly disturbs any of those fauna, and

> (b) knew that what he destroyed, damaged or disturbed was within a site of special scientific interest,

is guilty of an offence and is liable on summary conviction to a fine not exceeding £20,000 or on conviction on indictment to a fine.

(7) It is a reasonable excuse in any event for a person to do what is mentioned in subsection (6) if—

> (a) paragraph (a) or (b) of subsection (4) is satisfied in relation to what was done (reading references there to an operation as references to the destruction, damage or disturbance referred to in subsection (6)), and

> (b) where appropriate, subsection (5) is also satisfied, reading the reference there to an operation in the same way.

(8) A person who without reasonable excuse fails to comply with a requirement of a management notice is guilty of an offence and is liable on summary conviction to a fine not exceeding the statutory maximum or on conviction on indictment to a fine.

(9) In determining the amount of any fine to be imposed on a person convicted of an offence under this section, the court shall in particular have regard to any financial benefit which has accrued or appears likely to accrue to him in consequence of the offence.

(10) Proceedings in England and Wales for an offence under this section shall not, without the consent of the Director of Public Prosecutions, be taken by a person other than the Council.

(11) In this section, "a section 28G authority" means an authority to which section 28G applies.

Change of owner or occupier.

28Q.—(1) This section applies where the owner of land included in a site of special scientific interest—

(a) disposes of any interest of his in the land; or

(b) becomes aware that it is occupied by an additional or a different occupier.

(2) If this section applies, the owner shall send a notice to the Nature Conservancy Council before the end of the period of 28 days beginning with the date on which he disposed of the interest or became aware of the change in occupation.

(3) The notice is to specify the land concerned and—

(a) in a subsection (1)(a) case, the date on which the owner disposed of the interest in the land, and the name and address of the person to whom he disposed of the interest; or

(b) in a subsection (1)(b) case, the date on which the change of occupation took place (or, if the owner does not know the exact date, an indication of when to the best of the owner's knowledge it took place), and, as far as the owner knows them, the name and address of the additional or different occupier.

(4) A person who fails without reasonable excuse to comply with the requirements of this section is guilty of an offence and is liable on summary conviction to a fine not exceeding level 1 on the standard scale.

(5) For the purposes of subsection (1), an owner "disposes of" an interest in land if he disposes of it by way of sale, exchange or lease, or by way of the creation of any easement, right or privilege, or in any other way except by way of mortgage.

Byelaws.

28R.—(1) The Nature Conservancy Council may make byelaws for the protection of a site of special scientific interest.

(2) The following provisions of the 1949 Act apply in relation to byelaws under this section as they apply in relation to byelaws under section 20 of that Act—

(a) subsections (2) and (3) of section 20 (reading references there to nature reserves as references to sites of special scientific interest); and

(b) sections 106 and 107."

2. Section 29 (special protection for certain areas of special scientific interest) and section 30 (compensation where an order is made under section 29) of the 1981 Act shall cease to have effect.

3.—(1) Section 31 of the 1981 Act (restoration where order under section 29 is contravened) is amended as follows.

(2) For subsection (1) there is substituted—

"(1) Where—

(a) the operation in respect of which a person is convicted of an offence under section 28P(1), (2) or (3) has destroyed or damaged any of the flora, fauna or geological or physiographical features by reason of which a site of special scientific interest is of special interest, or

(b) a person is convicted of an offence under section 28P(6),

the court by which he is convicted, in addition to dealing with him in any other way, may make an order requiring him to carry out, within such period as may be specified in the order, such operations (whether on land included in the site of special scientific interest or not) as may be so specified for the purpose of restoring the site of special scientific interest to its former condition."

(3) For the sidenote, there is substituted "Restoration following offence under section 28P.".

4. In section 32 (duties of agriculture Ministers with respect to areas of special scientific interest), in subsection (1), for "land notified under section 28(1)" there is substituted "land included in a site of special scientific interest".

5.—(1) Section 52 of the 1981 Act (interpretation of Part II) is amended as follows.

(2) In subsection (1), after the definition of "the Nature Conservancy Councils" there is inserted—

""notice" and "notification" mean notice or notification in writing;

"site of special scientific interest" means an area of land which has been notified under section 28(1)(b);".

(3) In subsection (2), after "district planning authority" there is inserted "and, in sections 28 to 28D, shall also be construed in accordance with section 28(10);".

(4) After subsection (2) there is inserted—

"(2A) Where a notification under section 28(1)(b) has been—

(a) modified under section 28(5)(b),

(b) varied under section 28A(3), or

(c) varied with modifications under section 28A(5)(b),

(d) extended under section 28B(2), or

(e) extended with modifications by virtue of section 28B(7),

a reference to such a notification (however expressed) is (unless the context otherwise requires) a reference to the notification as thus altered.

(2B) References to a notification under section 28(1) or 28(5)(b), or to a local land charge existing by virtue of section 28(9), shall be construed in accordance with section 28C(9).

(2C) For the purposes of this Part, in relation to land in England and Wales which is common land, "occupier" includes the commoners or any of them; and

(a) "common land" means common land as defined in section 22 of the Commons Registration Act 1965; and   1965 c. 64.

(b) "commoner" means a person with rights of common as defined in that section."

6. In section 67 of the 1981 Act (application to Crown), after subsection (1) there is inserted—

"(1A) An interest in Crown land, other than one held by or on behalf of the Crown, may be acquired under section 28N, but only with the consent of the appropriate authority.

(1B) Byelaws made by virtue of section 28R may apply to Crown land if the appropriate authority consents."

7. In the 1981 Act, after Schedule 10 there is inserted the following Schedule—

"SCHEDULE 10A

DELEGATION OF APPELLATE FUNCTIONS

Interpretation

1. In this Schedule—

"appointed person" means a person appointed under section 28F(8) or 28L(10); and

"appointment", in the case of any appointed person, means appointment under either of those provisions.

Appointments

2. An appointment under section 28F(8) or 28L(10) must be in writing and—

(a) may relate to any particular appeal or matter specified in the appointment or to appeals or matters of a description so specified;

(b) may provide for any function to which it relates to be exercisable by the appointed person either unconditionally or subject to the fulfilment of such conditions as may be specified in the appointment; and

(c) may, by notice in writing given to the appointed person, be revoked at any time by the Secretary of State in respect of any appeal or matter which has not been determined by the appointed person before that time.

Powers of appointed person

3. Subject to the provisions of this Schedule, an appointed person shall, in relation to any appeal or matter to which his appointment relates, have the same powers and duties as the Secretary of State, other than—

(a) any function of making regulations;

(b) any function of holding an inquiry or other hearing or of causing an inquiry or other hearing to be held; or

(c) any function of appointing a person for the purpose—

(i) of enabling persons to appear before and be heard by the person so appointed, or

(ii) of referring any question or matter to that person.

Holding of local inquiries and other hearings by appointed persons

4.—(1) If either of the parties to an appeal or matter expresses a wish to appear before and be heard by the appointed person, the appointed person shall give both of them an opportunity of appearing and being heard.

(2) Whether or not a party to an appeal or matter has asked for an opportunity to appear and be heard, the appointed person—

(a) may hold a local inquiry or other hearing in connection with the appeal or matter, and

(b) shall, if the Secretary of State so directs, hold a local inquiry in connection with the appeal or matter.

(3) Where an appointed person holds a local inquiry or other hearing by virtue of this Schedule, an assessor may be appointed by the Secretary of State to sit with the appointed person at the inquiry or hearing and advise him on any matters arising, notwithstanding that the appointed person is to determine the appeal or matter.

(4) Subject to section 28F(10) or 28L(12), the costs of a local inquiry held under this Schedule shall be defrayed by the Secretary of State.

Revocation of appointments and making of new appointments

5.—(1) Where under paragraph 2(c) the appointment of the appointed person is revoked in respect of any appeal or matter, the Secretary of State shall, unless he proposes to determine the appeal or matter himself, appoint another person under section 28F(8) or 28L(10) to determine the appeal or matter instead.

(2) Where such a new appointment is made, the consideration of the appeal or matter, or any hearing in connection with it, shall be begun afresh.

(3) Nothing in sub-paragraph (2) shall require any person to be given an opportunity of making fresh representations or modifying or withdrawing any representations already made.

Certain acts and omissions of appointed persons to be treated as those of the Secretary of State

6.—(1) Anything done or omitted to be done by an appointed person in, or in connection with, the exercise or purported exercise of any function to which the appointment relates shall be treated for all purposes as done or omitted to be done by the Secretary of State.

(2) Sub-paragraph (1) shall not apply—

(a) for the purposes of so much of any contract made between the Secretary of State and the appointed person as relates to the exercise of the function; or

(b) for the purposes of any criminal proceedings brought in respect of anything done or omitted to be done as mentioned in that sub-paragraph."

SCHEDULE 10

Section 76(1).

CONSEQUENTIAL AMENDMENTS RELATING TO SITES OF SPECIAL SCIENTIFIC INTEREST

PART I

AMENDMENTS OF WILDLIFE AND COUNTRYSIDE ACT 1981

1.—(1) The 1981 Act is amended as follows.

(2) In section 28 (areas of special scientific interest)—

(a) in subsection (8)(a), "Part III of the Town and Country Planning Act 1990 or" is omitted; and

(b) subsections (10) and (11) are omitted.

(3) In section 29 (special protection for certain areas of special scientific interest), in subsection (9)(a), "Part III of the Town and Country Planning Act 1990 or" is omitted.

(4) In section 30 (compensation where order is made under section 29)—

(a) in subsection (4)(c), "section 10 of the Land Compensation Act 1973 (mortgages, trusts for sale and settlements) or" is omitted;

(b) in subsection (5), "section 5 of the Land Compensation Act 1961 or" is omitted;

(c) in subsection (7), "section 32 of the Land Compensation Act 1961 or" is omitted;

(d) in subsection (8), "the Lands Tribunal or" is omitted; and

(e) in subsection (9), "sections 2 and 4 of the Land Compensation Act 1961 or" is omitted.

2. In section 74 of the 1981 Act (short title, commencement and extent), after subsection (5) there is inserted—

"(5A) Sections 29 and 30 extend to Scotland only."

PART II
OTHER AMENDMENTS
Harbours Act 1964 (c. 40)

3. In Schedule 3 to the Harbours Act 1964 (procedure for making harbour revision and empowerment orders), in paragraph 1 (interpretation), for paragraph (a) of the definition of "sensitive area" there is substituted—

"(a) land within a site of special scientific interest (within the meaning of the Wildlife and Countryside Act 1981);".

Conservation of Seals Act 1970 (c. 30)

4. In section 10 of the Conservation of Seals Act 1970 (power to grant licences to kill or take seals), in subsection (4), for paragraph (b) there is substituted—

"(b) is a site of special scientific interest (within the meaning of the Wildlife and Countryside Act 1981); or".

1981 c. 69.

Highways Act 1980 (c. 66)

5. In section 105A of the Highways Act 1980 (environmental impact assessments), in subsection (6), for paragraph (a) there is substituted—

"(a) a site of special scientific interest (within the meaning of the Wildlife and Countryside Act 1981);".

Channel Tunnel Act 1987 (c. 53)

6. In section 9 of the Channel Tunnel Act 1987 (planning permission), for subsection (7) there is substituted—

"(7) Section 28I of the Wildlife and Countryside Act 1981 (statutory undertakers: duty in relation to authorising operations) shall not apply in relation to any operation which is connected with the carrying out of any works authorised to be carried out by this Act and which is carried out within the limits of land to be acquired for any of those works, and neither shall the following—

(a) section 28E(1) (prohibition of operations on land forming part of a site of special scientific interest), in relation to an owner or occupier other than an authority to which section 28G of that Act applies;

(b) sections 28G(2) (general duty of statutory undertakers) and 28H (duty of statutory undertakers when carrying out operations), in relation to such an authority."

Town and Country Planning Act 1990 (c. 8)

7. In section 87 of the Town and Country Planning Act 1990 (exclusion of certain descriptions of land or development from a simplified planning zone), in subsection (1), for paragraph (f) there is substituted—

"(f) land within a site of special scientific interest (within the meaning of the Wildlife and Countryside Act 1981).".

Environmental Protection Act 1990 (c. 43)

8. In section 36 of the Environmental Protection Act 1990 (grant of waste management licences), in subsection (7), for "land which has been notified under section 28(1) of the Wildlife and Countryside Act 1981 (protection for certain areas)" there is substituted "within a site of special scientific interest (within the meaning of the Wildlife and Countryside Act 1981)".

Water Industry Act 1991 (c. 56)

9. In section 156 of the Water Industry Act 1991 (restriction on disposals of land), in subsection (8), for paragraph (b) in the definition of "area of outstanding natural beauty or special scientific interest" there is substituted—

"(b) is a site of special scientific interest within the meaning of the Wildlife and Countryside Act 1981;".

Environment Act 1995 (c. 25)

10. In Schedule 13 to the Environment Act 1995 (review of old mineral planning permissions), for paragraph 2(4)(b) there is substituted—

"(b) a site of special scientific interest (within the meaning of the Wildlife and Countryside Act 1981);".

Channel Tunnel Rail Link Act 1996 (c. 61)

11. In Schedule 10 to the Channel Tunnel Rail Link Act 1996 (disapplication and modification of miscellaneous controls), for paragraph 6 and the heading preceding it there is substituted—

Sites of special scientific interest

6. Section 28I of the Wildlife and Countryside Act 1981 (statutory undertakers: duty in relation to authorising operations) shall not apply to any operation carried out for the purposes of or in connection with the exercise of any of the powers conferred by this Part of this Act with respect to works, and neither shall the following—   1981 c. 69.

(a) section 28E(1) (prohibition of operations on land forming part of a site of special scientific interest), in relation to an owner or occupier other than an authority to which section 28G of that Act applies;

(b) sections 28G(2) (general duty of statutory undertakers) and 28H (duty of statutory undertakers when carrying out operations), in relation to such an authority.".

SCHEDULE 11   Section 76(2).

Tʀᴀɴsɪᴛɪᴏɴᴀʟ ᴘʀᴏᴠɪsɪᴏɴs ᴀɴᴅ sᴀᴠɪɴɢs ʀᴇʟᴀᴛɪɴɢ ᴛᴏ sɪᴛᴇs ᴏғ sᴘᴇᴄɪᴀʟ
sᴄɪᴇɴᴛɪғɪᴄ ɪɴᴛᴇʀᴇsᴛ

Interpretation

1.—(1) In this Schedule—

"the Nature Conservancy Council" has the meaning given by section 27A of the 1981 Act and "stop notice" has the meaning given by paragraph 9(3) of this Schedule;

"old section 28" means section 28 of the 1981 Act as it had effect before its substitution by section 75(1) of and Schedule 9 to this Act;

"new section 28" means section 28 of the 1981 Act as substituted by section 75(1) of and Schedule 9 to this Act; and

"the substitution date" means the date on which new section 28 is substituted for old section 28,

and references to other sections are to those sections in the 1981 Act unless otherwise specified.

1978 c. 30.
(2) Nothing in this Schedule prejudices the application of section 16 (general savings) or 17 (repeal and re-enactment) of the Interpretation Act 1978 to any case not provided for in this Schedule.

Notifications given under old section 28

2. Except as mentioned in paragraphs 4 and 5, a notification under old section 28(1)(a), (b) or (c) (including one having effect in modified form by virtue of old section 28(4C)) has effect from the substitution date as if it were a notification under new section 28(1)(a), (b) or (c) respectively.

3. A notice under old section 28(4A)(a) or (b) has effect from the substitution date as if it were a notice under new section 28(5)(a) or (b) respectively.

Modification of operation of new section 28

4. New section 28(2) does not apply to a notification taking effect as mentioned in paragraph 2.

5. The words following paragraph (b) in new section 28(4) do not apply to a notification taking effect as mentioned in paragraph 2, but instead paragraph 6 applies.

6.—(1) The Nature Conservancy Council shall, within the period of five years beginning with the substitution date, give a notice to every owner and occupier of any land which is the subject of—

(a) a notification under old section 28(4A)(b), or

(b) a notice under new section 28(5)(b) following a notification under old section 28(1),

containing a statement of the Council's views about the matters referred to in the words following paragraph (b) in new section 28(4).

(2) The notice shall specify the date (not being less than three months from the date of the giving of the notice) on or before which, and the manner in which, representations or objections with respect to it may be made; and the Council shall consider any representation or objection duly made.

(3) Within the period of two months beginning immediately after the date referred to in sub-paragraph (2), the Council shall give a notice to every owner and occupier of the land confirming the statement referred to in sub-paragraph (1) or containing a revised statement.

Modification of operation of section 28A

7.—(1) This paragraph applies to a notification under old section 28(1) given—

1985 c. 31.
(a) before the commencement of the Wildlife and Countryside (Amendment) Act 1985; or

(b) after the commencement of that Act but preceded by a notice under section 28(2) as originally enacted, given during the six months immediately preceding that commencement.

(2) In relation to a notification to which this paragraph applies, the reference in section 28A(1) to—

(a) notice given under section 28(5)(b) confirming a notification with or without modifications, and

(b) the confirmed notification,

shall be construed as a reference to the notification under old section 28(1).

Modification of operation of section 28E

8.—(1) Except as provided in paragraph 9—

(a) a notice given under old section 28(5)(a) has effect from the substitution date as if it were a notice given under section 28E(1)(a); and

(b) a consent given under old section 28(6)(a) has effect from that date as if it were a consent under section 28E(3)(a).

(2) In relation to such a consent, section 28E has effect as if for subsections (7) and (8) there were substituted—

"(7) A notice under subsection (6) must include a notice of—

(a) the Council's reasons for withdrawing or modifying the consent;

(b) the rights of appeal under section 28F;

(c) the effect of subsection (9); and

(d) the effect of section 28M."

9.—(1) Subject to paragraph 10, this paragraph applies where—

(a) a notice has been given under old section 28(5)(a) before the substitution date;

(b) on the substitution date neither of the conditions set out in old section 28(6)(a) and (b) is fulfilled; and

(c) on the substitution date four months have expired since the notice under old section 28(5)(a) was given,

but even if those conditions are fulfilled, this paragraph does not apply in relation to operations specified in a notice under section 29(4)(a) on any land if immediately before the substitution date an order under section 29 was in effect in relation to that land.

(2) Where this paragraph applies, but subject to sub-paragraph (7), the prohibition in section 28E(1) on carrying out, or causing or permitting to be carried out, an operation does not apply in relation to an operation specified in the notice under old section 28(5)(a).

(3) Where this paragraph applies, the Nature Conservancy Council may, on or after the substitution date, give a notice (a "stop notice") to every owner and occupier of the land to which the stop notice is to apply.

(4) A stop notice is to specify—

(a) the date on which it is to take effect;

(b) the operations to which it applies; and

(c) the land to which it applies,

and must contain a notice of the right of the person to whom the stop notice is given to appeal against it in accordance with paragraph 11, and a notice of the effect of sub-paragraph (8).

(5) The date on which a stop notice is to take effect may not be sooner than the end of the period of three days beginning with the date the stop notice is given, unless the Council consider that there are special reasons which justify a shorter period, and a statement of those reasons is included with the stop notice.

(6) The operations to which a stop notice may apply are all or any of the operations specified in the notice under old section 28(5)(a).

(7) From the date on which the stop notice takes effect, sub-paragraph (2) of this paragraph ceases to apply in relation to the operations specified in the stop notice on the land to which the stop notice applies.

(8) Where the Council give a stop notice, they shall make a payment to any owner or occupier of the land who suffers loss because of it.

(9) The amount of a payment under sub-paragraph (8) is to be determined by the Council in accordance with guidance given and published by the Ministers (within the meaning of section 50).

(10) Section 50(3) applies to the determination of the amount of a payment under sub-paragraph (8) as it applies to the determination of the amount of payments under that section.

(11) This paragraph ceases to apply, in relation to any operation specified in the notice referred to in sub-paragraph (1)(a) except an operation to which a stop notice applies, if the operation has not begun before the end of the period of—

    (a) three years beginning with the substitution date; or

    (b) in a case falling within paragraph 10(2) or (3), three years beginning immediately after the expiry of the period of one month or longer referred to there.

10.—(1) An agreement under old section 28(6A) in effect immediately before the substitution date has effect from the substitution date as an agreement that paragraph 9 is not to apply in relation to the operation which is the subject of the agreement; and, accordingly, paragraph 9 does not apply in relation to that operation (as regards both the owner and the occupier of the land).

(2) Where a notice has been given under old section 28(6B) before the substitution date, paragraph 9 has effect, in relation to the operation in question, as if for the period mentioned in paragraph 9(1)(c) there were substituted the period of one month from the giving of the notice or (if a longer period is specified in the notice) that longer period.

(3) If after an agreement has taken effect as mentioned in sub-paragraph (1) the relevant person (whether a party to the agreement or not) gives the Nature Conservancy Council written notice that he wishes to terminate the agreement, then as from the giving of the notice paragraph 9 has effect, in relation to the operation in question (as regards both the owner and the occupier of the land), as if for the period mentioned in paragraph 9(1)(c) there were substituted the period of one month from the giving of the notice or (if a longer period is specified in the notice) that longer period.

(4) In sub-paragraph (3), "relevant person" has the same meaning as in old section 28(6C).

11.—(1) A person to whom a stop notice is given may by notice appeal against it to the Secretary of State, but meanwhile it remains in effect.

(2) Section 28F(3) to (11) shall apply in relation to such an appeal as they apply in relation to an appeal against a decision to withdraw a consent (see section 28F(1)(d)), but with the following modifications—

    (a) as if, in section 28F(3), for paragraphs (a) and (b) and the following words "or, in either case," there were substituted "within the period of two months beginning with the date of the stop notice, or"; and

(b) as if, for section 28F(5), there were substituted—

"(5) On determining the appeal, the Secretary of State may quash or affirm the stop notice; and if he affirms it, he may do so either in its original form or with the removal from it of such operations as he thinks fit, or in relation to such reduced area of land as he thinks fit."

12.—(1) The Nature Conservancy Council may, by notice given to every owner and occupier of land to which a stop notice applies, vary a stop notice by removing any operation to which it applies or reducing the area of land to which it applies.

(2) Where after giving a stop notice—

(a) the Council consent to an operation to which the stop notice applies;

(b) an operation to which it applies becomes one which may be carried out under the terms of an agreement under section 16 of the National Parks and Access to the Countryside Act 1949 or section 15 of the Countryside Act 1968; or

1949 c. 97.

1968 c. 41.

(c) an operation to which it applies becomes one which may be carried out in accordance with a management scheme under section 28J or a management notice under section 28K,

the stop notice shall be deemed to be varied accordingly by the removal from the stop notice of the operation in question in relation to the land to which the consent, agreement or management scheme or notice relates.

Modification of operation of section 28F

13.—(1) Section 28F(1)(a) does not apply to a refusal of a consent under old section 28(6)(a).

(2) Section 28F(1)(b) does not apply to consents taking effect as mentioned in paragraph 8(1)(b).

Modification of operation of section 28H

14. Section 28H does not apply in relation to operations which have already begun on the date section 28H comes into force.

Section 29

15. Paragraphs 16 and 17 apply where, immediately before the coming into force of paragraph 2 of Schedule 9 to this Act, there is in effect an order applying section 29(3) to any land ("the relevant land").

16.—(1) If the relevant land is not included in a site of special scientific interest, section 28E applies to it as if it were (and accordingly section 28P(1) applies also); and references in section 28E to a notification under section 28(1)(b) shall be construed as references to an order under section 29.

(2) Whether or not the relevant land is included in a site of special scientific interest, a notice given under section 29(4)(a) has effect as if it were a notice given under section 28E(1)(a), except as provided in paragraph 17.

(3) Whether or not the relevant land is included in a site of special scientific interest, a consent given under section 29(5)(a) has effect as if it were a consent given under section 28E(3)(a), and in relation to such a consent section 28E has effect as if for subsections (7) and (8) there were substituted—

"(7) A notice under subsection (6) must include a notice of—

(a) the Council's reasons for withdrawing or modifying the consent;

(b) the rights of appeal under section 28F;

(c) the effect of subsection (9); and

(d) the effect of section 28M."

17.—(1) This paragraph applies where—

(a) a notice has been given under section 29(4)(a) before the repeal of section 29 by paragraph 2 of Schedule 9 to this Act;

(b) on the date on which paragraph 2 of Schedule 9 to this Act comes into force, neither of the conditions set out in section 29(5)(a) and (b) is fulfilled; and

(c) on that date the period mentioned in paragraph (c) of section 29(5) (or in that paragraph as it has effect by virtue of section 29(6) or (7)) has expired.

(2) Where this paragraph applies, but subject to paragraph 9(7) as it has effect by virtue of sub-paragraph (3) of this paragraph, the prohibition in section 28E(1) on carrying out, or causing or permitting to be carried out, an operation does not apply in relation to an operation specified in the notice under section 29(4)(a).

(3) Paragraphs 9(3) to (11) and 11 of this Schedule apply also in relation to this paragraph, but as if—

(a) in those provisions references to a notice under old section 28(5)(a) were to a notice under section 29(4)(a); and

(b) the reference to "sub-paragraph (2)" in paragraph 9(7) were to sub-paragraph (2) of this paragraph.

18.—(1) This paragraph applies where—

(a) as a result of the coming into force of paragraph 2 of Schedule 9 to this Act, a local inquiry or a hearing (as mentioned in paragraph 4(1)(a) and (b) respectively of Schedule 11 to the 1981 Act) comes to an end, and

(b) an owner or occupier of land in relation to which an order under section 29 has been made has incurred expense in connection with opposing the order at the local inquiry or hearing.

(2) If this paragraph applies, the Nature Conservancy Council shall (subject to sub-paragraph (3)) pay a person's expenses referred to in paragraph (1)(b) to the extent that they are reasonable.

(3) The Council need not pay any such expenses unless the person—

(a) applies to the Council for such a payment; and

(b) satisfies the Council that he has incurred the expenses.

Compensation and grants

19.—(1) Despite its repeal by paragraph 2 of Schedule 9 to this Act, section 30 (compensation where order made under section 29) continues to apply in connection with an order made under section 29 before the coming into force of that paragraph.

(2) After the repeal of section 29 by that paragraph, section 32 (duties of agriculture Ministers with respect to areas of special scientific interest) continues to apply, in relation to an application under that section relating to land to which section 29(3) applied immediately before its repeal, as if that land were included in a site of special scientific interest.

Offences and restoration orders

20.—(1) Section 28P does not have effect in relation to an offence committed before the substitution date, but old section 28 or, as the case may be, section 29, has effect instead.

(2) In relation to an offence under section 29, section 31 as it had effect before the coming into force of paragraph 3 of Schedule 9 to this Act shall continue to apply.

Powers of entry

21. Section 51 (powers of entry) has effect on and after the substitution date as if, in subsection (1), after paragraph (m) there were inserted—

"(n) to determine whether or not to give or vary a stop notice;",

and as if, in subsection (2)(a), after "paragraphs (a) to (k)" there were inserted "and paragraph (n)".

Service of notices

22. Section 70A (service of notices) applies in relation to notices given under this Schedule as it applies in relation to notices and other documents required or authorised to be served or given under the 1981 Act.

SCHEDULE 12   Section 81(1).

AMENDMENTS RELATING TO PART I OF WILDLIFE AND COUNTRYSIDE ACT 1981

1. In section 1(5) of the 1981 Act (offence of intentional disturbance of wild birds) after "intentionally" there is inserted "or recklessly".

2. In section 3 of that Act (areas of special protection) in subsection (1)(c) for "the offender shall be liable to a special penalty" there is substituted "the offence shall be treated as falling within section 7(3A)".

3. In section 6 of that Act (sale etc. of live or dead wild birds, eggs etc.), in subsection (2) the words from "who is not" to "Secretary of State" are omitted.

4.—(1) In section 7 of that Act (registration etc. of certain captive birds), in subsection (3)(a), for "for which a special penalty is provided" there is substituted "which falls within subsection (3A)".

(2) After subsection (3) of that section there is inserted—

"(3A) The offences falling within this subsection are—

(a) any offence under section 1(1) or (2) in respect of—

(i) a bird included in Schedule 1 or any part of, or anything derived from, such a bird,

(ii) the nest of such a bird, or

(iii) an egg of such a bird or any part of such an egg;

(b) any offence under section 1(5) or 5;

(c) any offence under section 6 in respect of—

(i) a bird included in Schedule 1 or any part of, or anything derived from, such a bird, or

(ii) an egg of such a bird or any part of such an egg;

(d) any offence under section 8.".

5. In section 9 of that Act (protection of certain wild animals)—

(a) in subsection (4) after "intentionally" there is inserted "or recklessly", and

(b) after that subsection there is inserted—

"(4A) Subject to the provisions of this Part, if any person intentionally or recklessly disturbs any wild animal included in Schedule 5 as—

(a) a dolphin or whale (cetacea), or

(b) a basking shark (cetorhinus maximus),

he shall be guilty of an offence."

6. In section 16(3) of that Act (power to grant licences) for "and (4)" there is substituted ", (4) and (4A)".

7. In section 19 of that Act (enforcement of Part I), in subsection (3) for the words from "suspecting that" to "has been committed" there is substituted "suspecting that an offence under this Part has been committed".

8. After that section there is inserted—

"Enforcement: wildlife inspectors.   19ZA.—(1) In this Part, "wildlife inspector" means a person authorised in writing by the Secretary of State under this subsection.

(2) An authorisation under subsection (1) is subject to any conditions or limitations specified in it.

(3) A wildlife inspector may, at any reasonable time and (if required to do so) upon producing evidence that he is authorised—

(a) enter and inspect any premises for the purpose of ascertaining whether an offence under section 6, 9(5) or 13(2) is being, or has been, committed on those premises;

(b) enter and inspect any premises where he has reasonable cause to believe that any birds included in Schedule 4 are kept, for the purpose of ascertaining whether an offence under section 7 is being, or has been, committed on those premises;

(c) enter any premises for the purpose of ascertaining whether an offence under section 14 is being, or has been, committed on those premises;

(d) enter and inspect any premises for the purpose of verifying any statement or representation which has been made by an occupier, or any document or information which has been furnished by him, and which he made or furnished—

(i) for the purposes of obtaining (whether for himself or another) a relevant registration or licence, or

(ii) in connection with a relevant registration or licence held by him.

(4) In subsection (3)—

(a) paragraphs (a) and (b) do not confer power to enter a dwelling except for purposes connected with—

(i) a relevant registration or licence held by an occupier of the dwelling, or

(ii) an application by an occupier of the dwelling for a relevant registration or licence; and

(b) paragraph (c) does not confer any power to enter a dwelling.

(5) A wildlife inspector may, for the purpose of ascertaining whether an offence under section 6, 7, 9(5), 13(2) or 14 is being, or has been, committed in respect of any specimen, require any person who has the specimen in his possession or control to make it available for examination by the inspector.

(6) Any person who has in his possession or control any live bird or other animal shall give any wildlife inspector acting in the exercise of powers conferred by this section such assistance as the inspector may reasonably require for the purpose of examining the bird or other animal.

(7) Any person who—

(a) intentionally obstructs a wildlife inspector acting in the exercise of powers conferred by subsection (3) or (5), or

(b) fails without reasonable excuse to give any assistance reasonably required under subsection (6),

shall be guilty of an offence.

(8) Any person who, with intent to deceive, falsely pretends to be a wildlife inspector shall be guilty of an offence.

(9) In this section—

"relevant registration or licence" means—

(a) a registration in accordance with regulations under section 7(1), or

(b) a licence under section 16 authorising anything which would otherwise be an offence under section 6, 7, 9(5), 13(2) or 14; and

"specimen" means any bird, other animal or plant or any part of, or anything derived from, a bird, other animal or plant.

Power to take samples.

19ZB.—(1) A constable who suspects with reasonable cause that a specimen found by him in the exercise of powers conferred by section 19 is one in respect of which an offence under this Part is being or has been committed may require the taking from it of a sample of blood or tissue in order to determine its identity or ancestry.

(2) A constable who suspects with reasonable cause that an offence under this Part is being or has been committed in respect of any specimen ("the relevant specimen") may require any person to make available for the taking of a sample of blood or tissue any specimen (other than the relevant specimen) in that person's possession or control which is alleged to be, or which the constable suspects with reasonable cause to be, a specimen a sample from which will tend to establish the identity or ancestry of the relevant specimen.

(3) A wildlife inspector may, for the purpose of ascertaining whether an offence under section 6, 7, 9(5), 13(2) or 14 is being or has been committed, require the taking of a sample of blood or tissue from a specimen found by him in the exercise of powers conferred by section 19ZA(3)(a) to (c) in order to determine its identity or ancestry.

(4) A wildlife inspector may, for the purpose of ascertaining whether an offence under section 6, 7, 9(5), 13(2) or 14 is being or has been committed in respect of any specimen ("the relevant specimen"), require any person to make available for the taking of a sample of blood or tissue any specimen (other than the relevant specimen) in that person's possession or control which is alleged to be, or which the wildlife inspector suspects with reasonable cause to be, a specimen a sample from which will tend to establish the identity or ancestry of the relevant specimen.

(5) No sample from a live bird, other animal or plant shall be taken pursuant to a requirement under this section unless the person taking it is satisfied on reasonable grounds that taking the sample will not cause lasting harm to the specimen.

(6) No sample from a live bird or other animal shall be taken pursuant to such a requirement except by a veterinary surgeon.

(7) Where a sample from a live bird or other animal is to be taken pursuant to such a requirement, any person who has possession or control of the specimen shall give the person taking the sample such assistance as he may reasonably require for that purpose.

(8) A constable entering premises under section 19(2), and any wildlife inspector entering premises under section 19ZA(3), may take with him a veterinary surgeon if he has reasonable grounds for believing that such a person will be required for the exercise on the premises of powers under subsections (1) to (4).

(9) Any person who—

(a) intentionally obstructs a wildlife inspector acting in the exercise of the power conferred by subsection (3),

(b) fails without reasonable excuse to make available any specimen in accordance with a requirement under subsection (2) or (4), or

(c) fails without reasonable excuse to give any assistance reasonably required under subsection (7),

shall be guilty of an offence.

(10) In this section—

(a) "specimen" has the same meaning as in section 19ZA, and

(b) in relation to a specimen which is a part of, or is derived from, a bird, other animal or plant, references to determining its identity or ancestry are to determining the identity or ancestry of the bird, other animal or plant."

9.—(1) In section 20 of that Act (time limit for summary prosecution of certain offences under Part I)—

(a) subsection (1) is omitted, and

(b) in subsection (2) for "an offence to which this section applies" there is substituted "an offence under this Part".

(2) Sub-paragraph (1) does not have effect in relation to any offence committed before the commencement of this paragraph.

10.—(1) Section 21 of that Act (penalties, forfeitures etc. for offences under Part I) is amended as follows.

(2) For subsections (1) to (3) there is substituted—

"(1) Subject to subsection (5), a person guilty of an offence under any of sections 1 to 13 or section 17 shall be liable on summary conviction to imprisonment for a term not exceeding six months or to a fine not exceeding level 5 on the standard scale, or to both."

(3) In subsection (4)—

(a) in paragraph (a) for the words from "to a fine" to the end there is substituted "to imprisonment for a term not exceeding six months or to a fine not exceeding the statutory maximum, or to both", and

(b) in paragraph (b) for "to a fine" there is substituted "to imprisonment for a term not exceeding two years or to a fine, or to both".

(4) After subsection (4) there is inserted—

"(4A) Except in a case falling within subsection (4B), a person guilty of an offence under section 19ZA(7) shall be liable on summary conviction to a fine not exceeding level 5 on the standard scale.

(4B) A person guilty of an offence under subsection (7) of section 19ZA in relation to a wildlife inspector acting in the exercise of the power conferred by subsection (3)(c) of that section shall be liable—

(a) on summary conviction, to a fine not exceeding the statutory maximum;

(b) on conviction on indictment, to a fine.

(4C) A person guilty of an offence under section 19ZA(8) shall be liable—

(a) on summary conviction, to imprisonment for a term not exceeding six months or a fine not exceeding the statutory maximum, or to both;

(b) on conviction on indictment, to imprisonment for a term not exceeding two years or to a fine, or to both.

(4D) A person guilty of an offence under section 19ZB(9) shall be liable on summary conviction to a fine not exceeding level 5 on the standard scale."

(5) In subsection (5) the words ", (2) or (3)" are omitted.

(6) Sub-paragraphs (1) to (5) and the repeal by this Act of provisions of the 1981 Act relating to special penalties do not have effect in relation to any offence committed before the commencement of this paragraph.

11. In section 24 of that Act (functions of the Nature Conservancy Councils), in subsection (4) for paragraph (c) there is substituted—

"(c) any wildlife inspector,".

12. In section 27 of that Act (interpretation of Part I), in subsection (1) after the definition of "wild plant" there is inserted—

""wildlife inspector" has the meaning given by section 19ZA(1)."

13. In section 24(2) of the Police and Criminal Evidence Act 1984 (arrestable offences), after paragraph (r) there is inserted—   1984 c. 60.

"(s) an offence under section 1(1) or (2) or 6 of the Wildlife and Countryside Act 1981 (taking, possessing, selling etc. of wild birds) in respect of a bird included in Schedule 1 to that Act or any part of, or anything derived from, such a bird;

(t) an offence under any of the following provisions of the Wildlife and Countryside Act 1981—

(i) section 1(5) (disturbance of wild birds),

(ii) section 9 or 13(1)(a) or (2) (taking, possessing, selling etc. of wild animals or plants),

(iii) section 14 (introduction of new species etc.)."

Section 86(2).

SCHEDULE 13

AREAS OF OUTSTANDING NATURAL BEAUTY: CONSERVATION BOARDS

Interpretation

1. In this Schedule—

"an English conservation board" means a conservation board for an area of outstanding natural beauty in England;

"the relevant order", in relation to a conservation board, means—

(a) the order under section 86 establishing that board,

(b) any order under that section relating to that board, or

(c) any order made in relation to that board in exercise of the power to amend an order under that section.

Status and constitution of conservation boards

2. A conservation board shall be a body corporate.

3.—(1) A conservation board shall consist of—

(a) such number of local authority members as may be specified in the relevant order,

(b) such number of members to be appointed by the Secretary of State or the National Assembly for Wales as may be so specified, and

(c) in the case of an English conservation board, such number of parish members as may be so specified.

(2) The numbers specified in the relevant order for any conservation board in relation to the membership of the board must be such that—

(a) the number of local authority members is at least 40 per cent. of the total number of members, and

(b) in the case of an English conservation board, the number of parish members is at least 20 per cent. of the total number of members.

Local authority members

4.—(1) The local authority members of a conservation board shall be appointed in accordance with the provisions of the relevant order.

(2) The relevant order must provide either—

(a) for the local authority members to be appointed by such of the local authorities for areas wholly or partly comprised in the area of outstanding natural beauty as may be specified in or determined under the order ("the relevant councils"), or

(b) for the local authority members to be appointed by such of the relevant councils as may be determined in accordance with a scheme contained in the relevant order.

(3) A person shall not be appointed as a local authority member of a conservation board unless he is a member of a local authority the area of which is wholly or partly comprised in the relevant area of outstanding natural beauty; and, in appointing local authority members of a conservation board, a local

authority shall have regard to the desirability of appointing members of the authority who represent wards, or (in Wales) electoral divisions, situated wholly or partly within the relevant area of outstanding natural beauty.

(4) Subject to the following provisions of this Schedule and to the provisions of the relevant order, where a person who qualifies for his appointment by virtue of his membership of any local authority is appointed as a local authority member of a conservation board—

    (a) he shall hold office from the time of his appointment until he ceases to be a member of that authority; but

    (b) his appointment may, before any such cessation, be terminated for the purposes of, and in accordance with, sections 15 to 17 of the Local Government and Housing Act 1989 (political balance).

(5) Sub-paragraph (4)(a) shall have effect so as to terminate the term of office of a person who, on retiring from any local authority, immediately becomes such a member again as a newly elected councillor; but a person who so becomes a member again shall be eligible for re-appointment to the conservation board.

(6) The appointment of any person as a local authority member of a conservation board may provide that he is not to be treated for the purposes of sub-paragraph (4) as qualifying for his appointment by virtue of his membership of any local authority other than that specified in the appointment.

(7) In paragraph 2(1) of Schedule 1 to the Local Government and Housing Act 1989 (bodies to which appointments have to be made taking account of political balance), after paragraph (ba) there is inserted—

    "(bb) a conservation board established by order under section 86 of the Countryside and Rights of Way Act 2000;".

Parish members

5.—(1) The parish members of an English conservation board shall be appointed in accordance with the provisions of the relevant order, by—

    (a) the parish councils for parishes the whole or any part of which is comprised in the relevant area of outstanding natural beauty, and

    (b) the parish meetings of any of those parishes which do not have separate parish councils.

(2) A person shall not be appointed as a parish member of an English conservation board unless he is—

    (a) a member of the parish council for a parish the whole or any part of which is comprised in the relevant area of outstanding natural beauty, or

    (b) the chairman of the parish meeting of a parish—

        (i) which does not have a separate parish council, and

        (ii) the whole or any part of which is comprised in the relevant area of outstanding natural beauty.

(3) Subject to the following provisions of this Schedule and to the provisions of the relevant order, where a person who qualifies for his appointment by virtue of his membership of a parish council is appointed as a parish member of an English conservation board, he shall hold office from the time of his appointment until he ceases to be a member of that parish council.

(4) Subject to the following provisions of this Schedule and to the provisions of the relevant order, where a person who qualifies for his appointment by virtue of his being the chairman of a parish meeting is appointed as a parish member of an English conservation board, he shall hold office from the time of his appointment until he ceases to be the chairman of that parish meeting.

(5) Sub-paragraph (3) or (4) shall not have effect so as to terminate the term of office of a person who retires from a parish council, or ceases to be the chairman of a parish meeting, until such time as may be determined by the Secretary of State or the National Assembly for Wales in accordance with the relevant order.

(6) A person who—

(a) on retiring from a parish council, or

(b) on ceasing to be the chairman of a parish meeting,

becomes a member of the parish council again as a newly elected councillor or, as the case may be, is elected to succeed himself as chairman of any parish meeting is eligible for re-appointment to the conservation board at the time mentioned in sub-paragraph (5).

Members appointed by the Secretary of State or the National Assembly for Wales

6.—(1) Before appointing any person as a member of a conservation board, the Secretary of State shall consult the Agency.

(2) Before appointing any person as a member of a conservation board, the National Assembly for Wales shall consult the Council.

(3) Subject to the following provisions of this Schedule and to the provisions of the relevant order, a person appointed as a member of a conservation board by the Secretary of State or the National Assembly for Wales—

(a) shall hold office for such period of not less than one year nor more than three years as may be specified in the terms of his appointment; but

(b) on ceasing to hold office shall be eligible for re-appointment.

(4) The term of office of a person appointed by the Secretary of State or the National Assembly for Wales to fill such a vacancy in the membership of a conservation board as occurs where a person appointed by the Secretary of State or the Assembly ceases to be a member of the board before the end of his term of office may be for a period of less than one year if it is made to expire with the time when the term of office of the person in respect of whom the vacancy has arisen would have expired.

(5) Subject to the provisions of this Schedule and of the relevant order, a member of a conservation board appointed by the Secretary of State or the National Assembly for Wales shall hold office in accordance with the terms of his appointment.

Chairman and deputy chairman

7.—(1) The members of a conservation board shall elect, from amongst their members, both a chairman and a deputy chairman of the board.

(2) Subject to sub-paragraphs (3) and (4), the chairman and deputy chairman of a conservation board shall be elected for a period not exceeding one year; but a person so elected shall, on ceasing to hold office at the end of his term of office as chairman or deputy chairman, be eligible for re-election.

(3) A person shall cease to hold office as chairman or deputy chairman of a conservation board if he ceases to be a member of the board.

(4) Where a vacancy occurs in the office of chairman or deputy chairman of a conservation board, it shall be the duty of the members of that board to secure that the vacancy is filled as soon as possible.

Audit

8. In Schedule 2 to the Audit Commission Act 1998 (accounts subject to audit) in paragraph 1 after paragraph (j) there is inserted—

> "(jj) a conservation board established by order under section 86 of the Countryside and Rights of Way Act 2000;".

SCHEDULE 14

SUPPLEMENTAL POWERS OF CONSERVATION BOARDS

Section 87(6).

Interpretation

1. In this Schedule—

"common", "disposal" and "open space" have the same meaning as in the Town and Country Planning Act 1990;

1990 c. 8.

"relevant order" has the same meaning as in Schedule 13.

Power to acquire land

2.—(1) For the purposes of any of their functions under this or any other enactment, a conservation board may acquire by agreement any land, whether situated inside or outside their area of outstanding natural beauty.

(2) The reference in sub-paragraph (1) to acquisition by agreement is a reference to acquisition for money or money's worth as purchaser or lessee.

Power to dispose of land

3. Subject to paragraphs 4 to 6 and to the provisions of the relevant order, a conservation board may dispose, in any manner they wish, of land which is held by them but no longer required by them for the purposes of their functions.

4.—(1) Except with the consent of the Secretary of State (as respects England) or the National Assembly for Wales (as respects Wales), a conservation board may not—

(a) dispose under paragraph 3 of land which consists of or forms part of a common, or formerly consisted of or formed part of a common, and is managed by a local authority in accordance with a local Act,

(b) dispose under paragraph 3 of land, otherwise than by way of a short tenancy, for a consideration less than the best that can reasonably be obtained.

(2) For the purposes of this paragraph a disposal of land is a disposal by way of a short tenancy if it consists—

(a) of the grant of a term not exceeding seven years, or

(b) of the assignment of a term which at the date of the assignment has not more than seven years to run.

5. A conservation board may not dispose under paragraph 3 of any land consisting of or forming part of an open space unless before disposing of the land they cause notice of their intention to do so, specifying the land in question, to be advertised in two consecutive weeks in a newspaper circulating in the area in which the land is situated, and consider any objections to the proposed disposal which may be made to them.

6. Section 128 of the Local Government Act 1972 (consents to land transactions by local authorities) applies in relation to a conservation board as if a conservation board were a principal council and as if paragraphs 3 to 5 were contained in Part VII of that Act.")

1972 c. 70.

SCH. 14

Provisions as to charges

1989 c. 42.

7. In section 152(2) of the Local Government and Housing Act 1989 (provisions as to charges), after paragraph (ja) there is inserted—

"(jb) a conservation board established by order under section 86 of the Countryside and Rights of Way Act 2000;";

and section 151 of that Act (power to amend existing provisions as to charges) shall have effect as if references to an existing provision included references to any such provision as applied by or under Part IV of this Act.

Section 93.

SCHEDULE 15

AREAS OF OUTSTANDING NATURAL BEAUTY: CONSEQUENTIAL AMENDMENTS AND TRANSITIONAL PROVISIONS

PART I

CONSEQUENTIAL AMENDMENTS

National Parks and Access to the Countryside Act 1949 (c. 97)

1. In section 1 of the National Parks and Access to the Countryside Act 1949 (the Countryside Agency and the Countryside Council for Wales), in subsection (2)(a) after "National Parks or" there is inserted "under the Countryside and Rights of Way Act 2000".

2. In section 112(2) of that Act (provisions not applying to Epping Forest and Burnham Beeches), for "eighty-seven" there is substituted "eighty-nine".

3. In section 114(1) of that Act (interpretation), for the definition of "area of outstanding natural beauty" there is substituted—

""area of outstanding natural beauty" means an area designated under section 82 of the Countryside and Rights of Way Act 2000;".

Harbours Act 1964 (c. 40)

4. In Schedule 3 to the Harbours Act 1964, in paragraph 1, in paragraph (i) of the definition of "sensitive area" for "section 87 of the National Parks and Access to the Countryside Act 1949" there is substituted "section 82 of the Countryside and Rights of Way Act 2000".

Highways Act 1980 (c. 66)

5. In section 105A of the 1980 Act (environmental impact assessments), in subsection (6), for paragraph (e) there is substituted—

"(e) an area of outstanding beauty designated as such under section 82 of the Countryside and Rights of Way Act 2000.".

Derelict Land Act 1982 (c. 42)

6. In section 1 of the Derelict Land Act 1982 (powers of Secretary of State), in subsection (11), in the definition of "area of outstanding natural beauty" for "section 87 of the National Parks and Access to the Countryside Act 1949" there is substituted "section 82 of the Countryside and Rights of Way Act 2000".

Road Traffic Regulation Act 1984 (c. 27)

7. In section 22 of the Road Traffic Regulation Act 1984 (traffic regulation for special areas in the countryside), at the end of subsection (1)(a)(ii) there is inserted "designated as such under section 82 of the Countryside and Rights of Way Act 2000".

Housing Act 1985 (c. 68)

8. In section 37 of the Housing Act 1985 (restriction on disposal of dwelling-houses in National Parks, etc), in subsection (1)(b) for "section 87 of the National Parks and Access to the Countryside Act 1949" there is substituted "section 82 of the Countryside and Rights of Way Act 2000".

9. In section 157 of that Act (restriction on disposal of dwelling-houses in National Parks, etc), in subsection (1)(b) for "section 87 of the National Parks and Access to the Countryside Act 1949" there is substituted "section 82 of the Countryside and Rights of Way Act 2000".

Town and Country Planning Act 1990 (c. 8)

10. In section 87 of the Town and Country Planning Act 1990 (exclusion of certain descriptions of land or development from a simplified planning zone), in subsection (1)(d) for "section 87 of the National Parks and Access to the Countryside Act 1949" there is substituted "section 82 of the Countryside and Rights of Way Act 2000".

Environmental Protection Act 1990 (c. 43)

11. In section 130 of the Environmental Protection Act 1990 (countryside functions of Countryside Council for Wales), in subsection (2)(a) after "National Parks or" there is inserted "under the Countryside and Rights of Way Act 2000".

Water Industry Act 1991 (c. 56)

12. In section 156 of the Water Industry Act 1991 (restriction on disposals of land), in subsection (8), in paragraph (a) of the definition of "area of outstanding natural beauty or special scientific interest", for "for the purposes of the National Parks and Access to the Countryside Act 1949" there is substituted "under section 82 of the Countryside and Rights of Way Act 2000".

Environment Act 1995 (c. 25)

13. In Schedule 13 to the Environment Act 1995 (review of old mineral planning permissions), in paragraph 2(4)(c) for "section 87 of the National Parks and Access to the Countryside Act 1949" there is substituted "section 82 of the Countryside and Rights of Way Act 2000".

Housing Act 1996 (c. 52)

14. In section 13 of the Housing Act 1996 (restriction on disposal of houses in National Parks, etc), in subsection (1)(b) for "section 87 of the National Parks and Access to the Countryside Act 1949" there is substituted "section 82 of the Countryside and Rights of Way Act 2000".

PART II

TRANSITIONAL PROVISIONS

15. In this Part "commencement" means the commencement of section 82.

16. Any order under section 87 of the 1949 Act (designation of areas of outstanding natural beauty) which is in force immediately before commencement is to be taken to have been made under section 82 in accordance with the provisions of Part IV of this Act, and may be amended or revoked by an order under that section.

17. Any reference in any instrument or document (whenever made) to designation as an area of outstanding natural beauty under section 87 of the 1949

Sch. 15

Act or to an order under that section is, in relation to any time after commencement, to be taken to be a reference to designation as such an area under section 82 or to an order under that section.

18. Anything done before commencement in connection with a proposed order under section 87 of the 1949 Act is, as from commencement, to be taken to have been done in connection with a proposed order under section 82.

Section 102.

SCHEDULE 16

REPEALS

PART I

ACCESS TO THE COUNTRYSIDE

Chapter	Short title	Extent of repeal
1925 c. 20.	The Law of Property Act 1925.	Section 193(2).
1949 c. 97.	The National Parks and Access to the Countryside Act 1949.	Sections 61 to 63. In section 111A(3)(a), the words "61 to 63,".
1972 c. 70.	The Local Government Act 1972.	In Schedule 17, paragraphs 35 and 35A.
1980 c. 65.	The Local Government, Planning and Land Act 1980.	In Schedule 3, paragraph 6.
1985 c. 51.	The Local Government Act 1985.	In Schedule 3, paragraph 5(9).
1990 c. 43.	The Environmental Protection Act 1990.	In Schedule 8, in paragraph 1(8), the words "62(1) and".
1994 c. 19.	The Local Government (Wales) Act 1994.	In Schedule 6, paragraph 13.

PART II

PUBLIC RIGHTS OF WAY AND ROAD TRAFFIC

Chapter	Short title	Extent of repeal
1980 c. 66.	The Highways Act 1980.	Section 134(5).
1981 c. 69.	The Wildlife and Countryside Act 1981.	Section 54. Section 56(5). In section 57(1), the words "on such scale as may be so prescribed,". In Schedule 15, paragraph 9.
1984 c. 27.	The Road Traffic Regulation Act 1984.	In section 22(1)(a), the words "(other than Greater London)" and, at the end of paragraph (vi), the word "or".

Chapter	Short title	Extent of repeal
1992 c. 42.	The Transport and Works Act 1992.	In Schedule 2, paragraphs 5(2), (4)(a), (d) and (e), (6) and (7), 6(2)(b) and 10(4)(a).

PART III

SITES OF SPECIAL SCIENTIFIC INTEREST

Chapter	Short title	Extent of repeal
1958 c. 51.	The Public Records Act 1958.	In Schedule 1, in Part II of the Table in paragraph 3, the entry relating to the Nature Conservancy Council for England.
1964 c. 40.	The Harbours Act 1964.	In Schedule 3, in the definition of "sensitive area", paragraph (b).
1965 c. 74.	The Superannuation Act 1965.	In section 39(1), in paragraph 7, the words "The Nature Conservancy Council for England.".
1967 c. 13.	The Parliamentary Commissioner Act 1967.	In Schedule 2, the entry "Nature Conservancy Council for England.
1970 c. 30.	The Conservation of Seals Act 1970.	Section 10(4)(c) and the following word "or".
1975 c. 24.	The House of Commons Disqualification Act 1975.	In Schedule 1, in Part III, the entry "Any member of the Nature Conservancy Council for England or the Countryside Council for Wales in receipt of remuncration.".
1980 c. 66.	The Highways Act 1980.	Section 105A(6)(c).
1981 c. 69.	The Wildlife and Countryside Act 1981.	Sections 29 and 30. In section 32(1), the words "or land to which section 29(3) applies". In section 67(2), the word "29,". In Schedule 11, in each of paragraphs 7(2) and 8, the words "29 or".
1985 c. 31.	The Wildlife and Countryside (Amendment) Act 1985.	Section 2.
1985 c. 59.	The Wildlife and Countryside (Service of Notices) Act 1985.	Section 1(2).

Chapter	Short title	Extent of repeal
1988 c. 4.	The Norfolk and Suffolk Broads Act 1988.	In Schedule 3, paragraph 31(1).
1990 c. 43.	The Environmental Protection Act 1990.	In Schedule 9, paragraph 11(9) to (11).
1996 c. 47.	The Trusts of Land and Appointment of Trustees Act 1996.	In Schedule 3, paragraph 20 and the heading preceding it.

PART IV

WILDLIFE

Chapter	Short title	Extent of repeal
1981 c. 69.	The Wildlife and Countryside Act 1981.	In section 1, subsection (4) and, in subsection (5), the words "and liable to a special penalty". In section 5(1), the words "and be liable to a special penalty". In section 6, in subsection (2) the words from "who is not" to "Secretary of State", and subsections (4) and (7) to (10). In section 7, in subsection (1) the words "and be liable to a special penalty", and subsections (6) and (7). In section 8, in subsections (1) and (3) the words "and be liable to a special penalty". Section 14(5) and (6). In section 17 the words "6(2) or". Section 20(1). In section 21(5) the words ", (2) or (3)".
1997 c. 55.	The Birds (Registration Charges) Act 1997.	Section 1(1).

PART V

AREAS OF OUTSTANDING NATURAL BEAUTY

Chapter	Short title	Extent of repeal
1949 c. 97.	The National Parks and Access to the Countryside Act 1949.	Sections 87 and 88.
1990 c. 43.	The Environmental Protection Act 1990.	In Schedule 8, paragraph 1(12).

Chapter	Short title	Extent of repeal
1995 c. 25.	The Environment Act 1995.	In Schedule 10, paragraph 2(7).

P<small>ART</small> VI
O<small>THER</small>

Chapter	Short title	Extent of repeal
1981 c. 69.	The Wildlife and Countryside Act 1981.	In section 39(1), the words "both in the countryside and".

Printed in the UK by The Stationery Office Limited
under the authority and superintendence of Carol Tullo, Controller of
Her Majesty's Stationery Office and Queen's Printer of Acts of Parliament

1st Impression December 2000
4th Impression August 2001